THE HENDERSON
illustrated anthology of
MONEY

EX LIBRIS

THE HENDERSON
illustrated anthology of
MONEY

**With money one may command devils:
Without it one cannot even summon a man.**

— *COMPILED BY* —
KRYSTYNA WEINSTEIN

curtis

TEXT ACKNOWLEDGEMENTS

Every effort has been made to secure permission to reproduce the following texts. We would like to thank the following publishers.
Penguin Books for: 60 words from *The Gambler* by Fyodor Dostoyevsky, transl. By J. Coulson (Penguin Classics, first published 1966), copyright ©J. Coulson 1966; 182 words from *Bel Ami* by Guy de Maupassant, transl. by D. Parmee (Penguin Classics, reprinted 1984), copyright ©D. Parmee 1976, 1980, 1982, 1984; 143 words from *Against Nature* by J-K Huysmans, transl. by R. Baldick (Penguin Classics, reprinted 1971), copyright ©R. Baldick 1959, 1966, 1968, 1971; 35 words from *Gargantua and Pantagruel* by François Rabelais, transl. by J.M. Cohen (Penguin Classics, reprinted 1963), copyright ©J.M. Cohen 1955, 1957, 1963; 25 lines from 'My purse, Gramercy to you for this' from *Celtic Miscellany,* transl. K.H. Jackson (Penguin Classics, reprinted 1984), copyright ©K.H. Jackson 1951, 1971; 13 lines from *The Canterbury Tales* by Geoffrey Chaucer, transl. by N. Coghill (Penguin Classics, revised edition 1977), copyright ©N. Coghill 1951, 1958, 1960, 1975, 1977; 331 words from *The Merchant of Prato* by Iris Origo (Peregrine Books, reprinted 1986), copyright ©Iris Origo 1957, 1963, 1979, 1986. Dover Publications for: 27 lines from *The Ship of Fools* by Sebastian Brant, transl. by Edwin H. Zeydel (1944). The *Independent* for: the theatre review of 'Serious Money', 30 March 1987. ©Times Newspapers Ltd for: Simon Jenkins, *The Sunday Times,* 25 October 1987; the leader, *The Times,* 25 July 1971; the theatre review, *The Sunday Times,* 29 March 1987. The *New York Times* for: article, 30 October 1929. Berkeley Publishing Group for: Paul Getty *How to be Rich* (1966). Unesco for: 'New Interpretations in the History of Banking' in R. de Roover *Banking and Economic Thought in Late Medieval and Early Modern Europe,* ed. J. Kirshner (1974). N.S. Behrman, *Duveen* (1953).

PICTURE ACKNOWLEDGEMENTS

We would like to thank the following: The Governor and Company of the Bank of England: pp 22, 23, 42, 54, 55, 73, 89; Bodleian Library, Oxford: p 33, Ms. Douce 134, fol. 95v; p 35, Ms. Douce 134 fol. 85; p 79, John Johnson Collection, South Sea Company; p 156, John Johnson Collection, Lotteries vol. 2; p 154, John Johnson Collection, sport II; p 157, John Johnson Collection, Lotteries Storage; Bruce Coleman Ltd: p 13; Cardiff City Council: p 127; Christies, London: p 135; Mary Evans Picture Library: pp 11, 19, 31, 40, 62, 92, 93, 99, 125, 137, 140, 151, 152/153; Fotomas Index: pp 8, 10, 81, 103, 121, 139; Guildhall Library, London: pp 38, 43, 46, 83, 115; Illustrated London News Picture Library: pp 45, 53, 56, 59, 149; Mansell Collection: p 27; Musée des Beaux Arts, Valenciennes: p 29; Museum of London: pp 49, 98, 116, 160; Peattie and Taylor: pp 67, 69; Popperfoto/Reuter: pp 57, 60, 107, 108, 126, 129; Punch: pp 15, 17, 64, 82, 102, 133, 142, 153; Royal Botanic Gardens, Kew: p 74; Gerald Scarfe: p 66, Sotheby's, London: p 130, 134, 135; Worthing Museum and Art Gallery: p 98

Produced by William Curtis Limited
83 Clerkenwell Road London EC1R 5AR

Editor John Collins
Design Jerry Goldie

British Library Cataloguing in Publication Data
The Henderson illustrated anthology of money.
1. Money.
I. Weinstein, Krystyna
332
ISBN 1 871967 05 8

Printed and bound by Richard Clay Ltd, Bungay, Suffolk

CONTENTS

'Gold and silver coins are only the tokens, symbols, outward and visible signs and sacraments of money. When not in the actual process of being applied in purchase, they are no more money than words not in use are language. Books are like imprisoned souls until someone takes them down from a shelf and reads them. The coins are potential money as the words are potential language; when the power and the will are in abeyance, the counters lie dead as a log.'

SAMUEL BUTLER, NOTEBOOKS (19th CENTURY)

FOREWORD

Amongst other old saws with which my father was wont to enlighten his children, he was given to telling us, "You can't buy experience with someone else's money".

I know exactly what he was trying to say, but I think it came of something as a shock to him when I confessed recently that I had been doing little else for twenty years.

As investment managers at Henderson Administration we spend our lives gaining experience in investments of all kinds, from stocks and shares to currency and unit trusts. We are always learning from the mountains of research work made available to us, the doors that are everywhere opened to us and the strange corners of the globe our task can take us to — all in the interest of looking after someone else's money. We certainly buy experience with it; hopefully we buy enough for our clients to benefit too.

The common language is money, whether yen, pfennig, lira or dirham in a multiplicity of forms, and this international language is as old as civilisation.

Krystyna Weinstein has researched into money in all its manifestations, into its attraction, humour, glitter, and power, and in so doing, has thrown an amusing light on its hold on man over the centuries. I will add only one quote from a fat file of anecdotes assembled over the years of working for a company where the sense of humour has rarely failed.

An elderly lady client had written to ask us for details of an annuity plan. The audio-typist's reply informed her that we would be delighted to provide her with details of 'a little naughty plan' for her ensuing years. One way or the other I like to think that she lived happily ever after.

Richard Henderson

CHAPTER I

— MONEY AS A MEANS OF EXCHANGE —

'I Promise to Pay the Bearer . . .'

Goats, camels, oxen, shells, fish, salt, iron, paper, silver and gold . . . ... these items have at one time or another been a form of money — a means of 'exchange'. In most instances they are items that had a universal high value placed on them — hence their use as 'currency'.

Paper is the exception. For paper money represents a 'promise' — to pay or to be further exchanged . And plastic, which at the press of a button disgorges money (even if it is only in paper form), is 20th-century alchemy and sorcery.

'. . . he gave me a reddish-grey powder. I dropped it into quicksilver in a crucible. I filled the crucible about half-way up with potash, put it over a gentle heat, and left it for about half an hour. When the crucible was red hot I threw a little piece of yellow wax into it. A few minutes later, I found a small piece of gold. It was melted in my presence and submitted to an assay: twenty-three carats fifteen grains of gold resulted, together with six of silver — both of an exceptionally bright colour . . .'

A 1603 account of transmuting metals.

> 'Against the talking power of money, eloquence is of no avail.'
>
> *ERASMUS, 15th/16th CENTURY*

In the Middle Ages it was believed that the Philosopher's Stone was the 'agent' which was capable of transforming base metals into gold and silver. Fire was the chief means of achieving the final transformation, once the alchemist had created his own stone from his own tested formula. Many alchemists sought patrons to further their success, for a tiny element of gold was necessary to start off the process.

One 13th-century alchemist, Pietro d'Apone, developed somewhat different money-gaining powers:

> **'. . . whenever he disbursed gold, he muttered a certain charm known only to himself and next morning the gold was safe again in his own possession. The trader to whom he gave it might lock it in his strong box and have it guarded by a troop of soldiers, but the charmed metal flew back to its old master . . . Few people in consequence liked to have dealings with such a personage . . . He was summoned before the tribunals of the Inquisition to answer for his crimes as a heretic and sorcerer . . . and died in prison.'**

François Rabelais, a loose-living French monk (born *c.* 1490), had the sharp tongue of a shrewd satirist and the wit of a gross-minded peasant. His famous giants – Gargantua and Pantagruel, and the latter's servant Panurge – are an exaggeration of the world that Rabelais saw around him, and parodied superbly.

Panurge was by nature subject to a malady that was called in those times 'the lack of money, pain incomparable' . . . yet when offered some, he disdained it.

> **"A fart for your money . . . I shall have more than I shall know what to do with one day. For my philosopher's stone draws me money out of purses as the magnet draws iron."**

. . . for he had 63 ways of obtaining money – the commonest and most honest of which was by cunning larceny. So when, asked Pantagruel, would he be out of debt?

> **"God forbid", he replied, "that I should ever be free of debt. For then I shall never find anyone to lend me a penny. A man who leaves no leaven overnight will never raise dough in the morning. Always owe something to someone. Then there will be prayers continually offered up to God to grant you a long and happy life. Through fear of losing his money, your creditor will even find new creditors for you. For by borrowing from them, you will repay him, and fill his ditch with other men's soil."**

'Come on sir. Now you set your foot on shore
In Novo Orbe; here's the rich Peru!
And there, within, sir, are the golden mines,
Great Solomon's Ophir.'

SIR EPICURE MAMMON IN BEN JONSON'S 'THE ALCHEMIST' (1612)

The Spaniards of the 15th and 16th centuries discovered that looting the gold used so lavishly in the South American kingdoms of the Aztecs and Incas was a more reliable way of obtaining the magical substance; they, and others, spent the next few decades seeking El Dorado — the seven cities of Cibola — fabled places where the streets were said to be paved of gold and the walls of houses adorned with rubies, sapphires and other precious jewels.

Money must have several qualities: it must be universally acceptable, universally exchangeable, and portable.

Homer's Greeks calculated value in terms of oxen: a bad bargain was struck when a suit of gold armour worth 100 oxen was exchanged for a bronze suit of armour worth only nine oxen.

Fifty years ago, goats were still currency in several East African countries; in 1620, salt was the money of the kingdoms of Upper Senegal and Upper Niger; and in Abyssinia the bars of rock salt used resembled those described by a 14th-century Arab traveller: 'the blacks use salt as gold and silver are used elsewhere. They cut it up into bits, and buy and sell with it'.

LORD BYRON

'They say that knowledge is power. I used to think so, but I now know they meant money . . . every guinea is a philosopher's stone . . . cash is a virtue.'

Sea shells have long been a form of money in coastal countries. The Portuguese found the zimbos — small sea snails — being used as currency in west Africa; and cowrie shells were widely used in countries bordering the Indian Ocean. Coral was until quite recently used in the interior of Nigeria; and the North American Indians' wampum — cylinders cut from shells — were still used by the first settlers until the mid-18th century. Many of them then turned to tobacco as a form of 'currency'.

Dried fish served the same purpose in 15th-century Iceland; furs were the common currency in parts of Peter the Great's Russia.

MONEY-COWRIES.

ADAM SMITH, WEALTH OF NATIONS (1776)

'A rich country, in the same manner as a rich man, is supposed to be a country abounding in money; and to heap up gold and silver in any country is supposed to be the readiest way to enrich it. For some time after the discovery of America, the first inquiry of the Spaniards, when they arrived upon any unknown coast, used to be if there was any gold or silver to be found in the neighbourhood? By the information which they received they judged whether it was worth while to make a settlement there, or if the country was worth conquering. Plano Carpino, a monk, sent as ambassador from the king of France to one of the sons of the famous Gengis Khan says that the Tartars used frequently to ask him if there were plenty of sheep and oxen in the kingdom of France? Their inquiry had the same object with that of the Spaniards. They wanted to know if the country was rich enough to be worth the conquering. Among the Tartars, as among all other nations of shepherds, who are generally ignorant of the use of money, cattle are the instruments of commerce and the measures of value. Wealth, therefore, according to them, consisted in cattle as according to the Spaniards, it consisted in gold and silver. Of the two, the Tartar notion, perhaps, was the nearer to the truth.'

'Nothing but money is sweeter than honey.'

BENJAMIN FRANKLIN, POOR RICHARD'S ALMANACK (1735)

BARTER

Barter — a basic means of exchange practised by all societies at one time or another — was still very prevalent in the early days of the American colonies. Two visiting Frenchmen remarked how: 'instead of money . . . it is the practice here for country folk to meet their needs by direct reciprocal exchange. The tailor and bootmaker do their work at the home of the farmer who requires it . . . he most frequently then provides the raw material for it and pays for the work in goods, keeping a written note of the value of the exchanges . . . at the end of the year the small quantity of coins is used to settle the differences.'

'All commodities exchanged must be able to be compared in some way. It is to meet this requirement that men have introduced money; money constitutes in a manner a middle term, for it is a measure of all things, and so of their superior or inferior value, that is to say, how many shoes are equivalent to a house or to a given quantity of food. As therefore a builder is to a shoemaker, so must such a number of shoes be to a house, or to a given amount of food; for without this reciprocal proportion, there can be no exchange and no association; and it cannot be secured unless the commodities in question be equal in a sense.

It is therefore necessary that all commodities shall be measured by some one standard, as was said before. And this standard is in reality demand, which is what holds everything together, since, if men cease to have wants or if either wants alter, exchange will go on no longer, or will be on different lines. But demand has come to be conventionally represented by money; this is why money is called nomisma (customary money) because it does not exist by nature but by custom (nomos), and can be altered and rendered useless at will.

ARISTOTLE, NICHOMACHEAN ETHICS

Trade without an accepted form of exchange became a great perplexity for one Philadelphia merchant in 1721: corn was no longer acceptable and money was in very short supply.

In 17th- and 18th-century Germany it was still the custom in country districts to pay weavers, miners and clock makers with salt, cloth, or measures of grain; and in 17th-century Japan it was common for herrings to be exchanged for loads of rice. A century earlier a more troublesome form of exchange in parts of the Caucasus were slaves: how to pay for daily expenses with such a commodity?

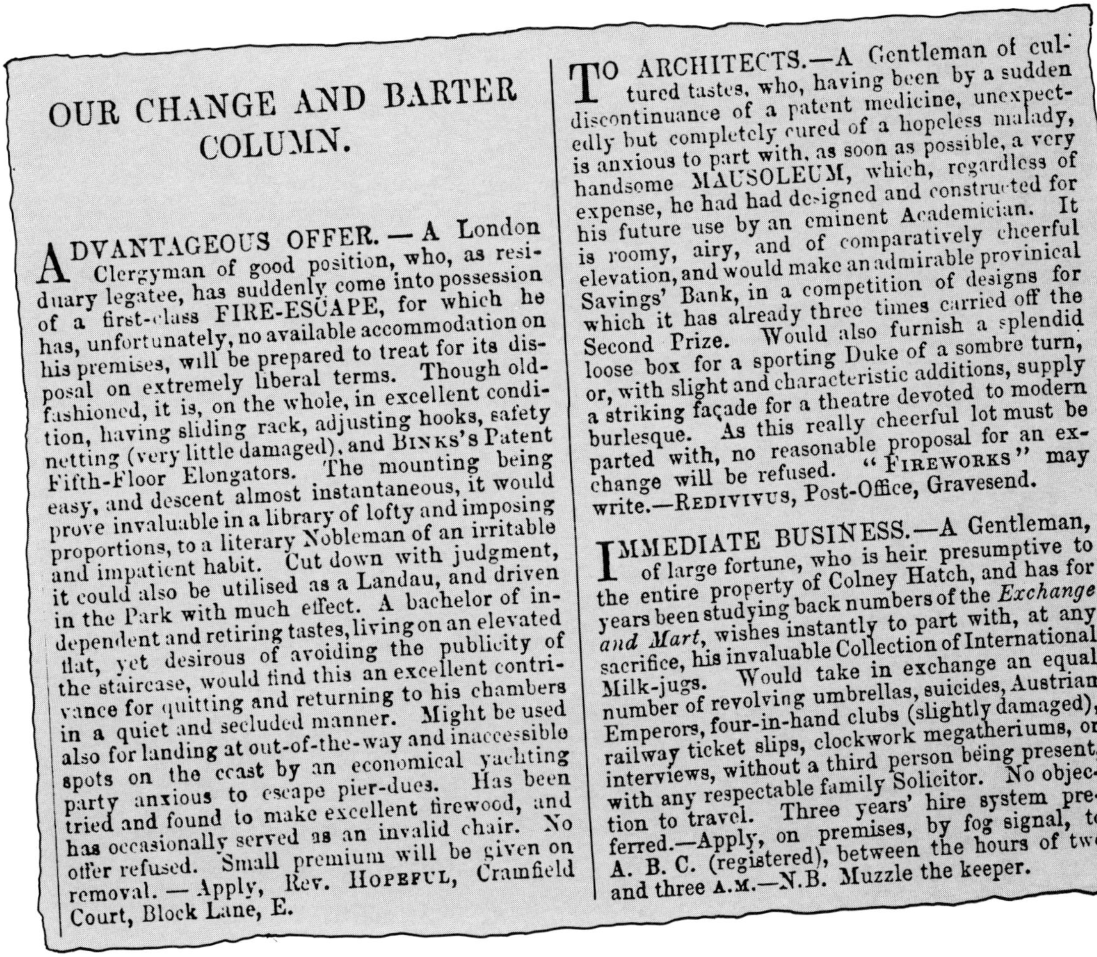

OUR CHANGE AND BARTER COLUMN.

ADVANTAGEOUS OFFER. — A London Clergyman of good position, who, as residuary legatee, has suddenly come into possession of a first-class FIRE-ESCAPE, for which he has, unfortunately, no available accommodation on his premises, will be prepared to treat for its disposal on extremely liberal terms. Though old-fashioned, it is, on the whole, in excellent condition, having sliding rack, adjusting hooks, safety netting (very little damaged), and BINKS's Patent Fifth-Floor Elongators. The mounting being easy, and descent almost instantaneous, it would prove invaluable in a library of lofty and imposing proportions, to a literary Nobleman of an irritable and impatient habit. Cut down with judgment, it could also be utilised as a Landau, and driven in the Park with much effect. A bachelor of independent and retiring tastes, living on an elevated flat, yet desirous of avoiding the publicity of the staircase, would find this an excellent contrivance for quitting and returning to his chambers in a quiet and secluded manner. Might be used also for landing at out-of-the-way and inaccessible spots on the coast by an economical yachting party anxious to escape pier-dues. Has been tried and found to make excellent firewood, and has occasionally served as an invalid chair. No offer refused. Small premium will be given on removal. — Apply, Rev. HOPEFUL, Cramfield Court, Block Lane, E.

TO ARCHITECTS.—A Gentleman of cultured tastes, who, having been by a sudden discontinuance of a patent medicine, unexpectedly but completely cured of a hopeless malady, is anxious to part with, as soon as possible, a very handsome MAUSOLEUM, which, regardless of expense, he had had designed and constructed for his future use by an eminent Academician. It is roomy, airy, and of comparatively cheerful elevation, and would make an admirable provincial Savings' Bank, in a competition of designs for which it has already three times carried off the Second Prize. Would also furnish a splendid loose box for a sporting Duke of a sombre turn, or, with slight and characteristic additions, supply a striking façade for a theatre devoted to modern burlesque. As this really cheerful lot must be parted with, no reasonable proposal for an exchange will be refused. "FIREWORKS" may write.—REDIVIVUS, Post-Office, Gravesend.

IMMEDIATE BUSINESS.—A Gentleman, of large fortune, who is heir presumptive to the entire property of Colney Hatch, and has for years been studying back numbers of the *Exchange and Mart*, wishes instantly to part with, at any sacrifice, his invaluable Collection of International Milk-jugs. Would take in exchange an equal number of revolving umbrellas, suicides, Austrian Emperors, four-in-hand clubs (slightly damaged), railway ticket slips, clockwork megatheriums, or interviews, without a third person being present, with any respectable family Solicitor. No objection to travel. Three years' hire system preferred.—Apply, on premises, by fog signal, to A. B. C. (registered), between the hours of two and three A.M.—N.B. Muzzle the keeper.

Punch's satirical 'Exchange and Mart' column, October 1881.

COINS

Electrum coins . . . easy to carry, durable, and worth their weight in gold and silver.

Electrum coins — ie, pieces made of mixed gold and silver, and stamped to guarantee their value — first appeared in 7th-century BC Lydia — now western Turkey. They earned Croesus, King of Lydia from 560-546 BC, his immortality.

The process spread throughout the Mediterranean world and beyond. The choice of subject for stamping is interesting for it conveyed a message about the 'issuer': many Lydian coins had lion and oxen heads, early Athenian ones had an owl — the symbol of Athene, the patroness of the city. Heads of rulers or their seals soon appeared on coinage, to lend credence and authority to the means of exchange.

One of the advantages of gold and silver coins was that they could be 'restruck' to the coinage of the land where a merchant was doing business: the facilities for minting such coins were to be found in all frontier towns of the Great Mogul's empire of China, and all foreign merchants were strongly advised to use them.

"Money?"
"Yes," said the child, laying his hands upon the elbows of his little chair, and turning the face up towards Mr Dombey's;
"what is money?"
Mr Dombey was in a difficulty. He would have liked to give him some explanation involving the terms circulating, medium, currency, depreciation of currency, paper, bullion, rates of exchange, value of precious metals in the market, and so forth; but looking down at the little chair, and seeing what a long way down it was, he answered: "gold, and silver and copper; guineas, shillings, half pence."

TEXT FROM DOMBEY & SON,

CHARLES DICKENS

ST. GEORGE AND THE DRAGON.

ENGLAND'S patron Saint has been summarily dismissed from the coin of the realm. ST. GEORGE and his Dragon have been ordered off in the most unceremonious manner, and have been superseded by the British Lion, with the QUEEN in the character of BRITANNIA, accompanied by that highly-favoured animal. This compliment to the British Lion is no doubt intended as a compensation for the many insults he has recently experienced.

We must not, however, pass over in silence the harsh and unfeeling treatment of the Dragon, who has for so many years given animation and spirit to our five-shilling pieces and our sovereigns. Poor ST. GEORGE will henceforth be ashamed to show his face among his companion champions of Christendom.

St George and the Dragon appeared on coins in the days of Henry VIII, only to be ousted albeit only temporarily, in the 19th century — an event much mourned by Punch.

In England in Anglo-Saxon times there were some 300 or 400 moneyers throughout the realm. They occasionally travelled with kings to coin money in emergencies. Their names appeared on their coins, which meant that makers of deficient coins could be easily traced.

Money was coined in eight places in London, seven in Canterbury, and in many other major cities. It was Henry II who put an end to the custom of barons, earls and bishops coining their own money. He became the sole source. In the reign of Elizabeth I, the Mint in the Tower became the only place to mint coins, except during the Civil War, when Charles II granted several cities the right to produce them.

The word 'money' is derived from 'Moneta', the cult name of Juno, in whose Temple in Rome coins were stamped out.

The word 'coin' derives from the French 'coign', a 'corner' . . . which might imply that early coins were squared off.

One wit disagreed, however:

'Why is the forme of money round?
Because it is to runne from every man.'

In 18th-century China, silver, not gold, was the most sought-after metal. Shaped in the form of small boats, these so-called 'loaves' were malleable enough to be cut up into smaller pieces depending on the size of the transaction. One European visitor in the 18th century described how:

> **'. . . there is scarcely a Chinaman, however wretched he may be, who does not carry scissors and a precision scale around with him. The former is used to cut gold and silver . . . the latter to weight the materials.'**

In England until the reign of James I, no standard weight was used for individual coins. Usually the law merely prescribed that a certain number should be cut from a pound of the metal. Owing to the unevenness of handiwork, there were not only differences in weight, but also in execution, as the force of the blows varied and consequently the impression on one coin was sometimes better than on another. Again, as edges were left unfinished, coins were clipped unmercifully, until a quarter or even a third of the metal had been abstracted, and people refused to take such 'light' money at its face value.

In the 16th century, the invention of the screw press enabled the upper die to be brought down by gradual pressure instead of by a series of blows from the hammer. This new process, first employed by Benvenuto Cellini, was introduced into the mint at Augsburg, and was thence brought to France, where so-called 'monnaie du moulin' was coined in the middle of the century. A few years later the mill and screw were introduced into England; but in both countries the new machinery was successfully opposed by the moneyers, whose craft was endangered, and consequently it was not permanently established in Paris until about 1640 or in London until some 20 years later.'

FRANCIS HIRST, MONEY, GOLD, SILVER AND PAPER (1931)

The TATLER

By *Ifaac Bickerftaff* Efq;

Per varios Cafus, per tot Difcrimina Rerum,
Tendimus. — — — Virg.

From *Thurfday November* 9. to *Saturday November* 11. 1710

From my own Apartment, November 10.

I was last night visited by a friend of mine who has an inexhaustible fund of discourse, and never fails to entertain his company with a variety of thoughts and hints that are altogether new and uncommon. Whether it were in complaisance to my way of living, or his real opinion, he advanced the following paradox, that it required much greater talents to fill up and become a retired life than a life of business. Upon this occasion he rallied very agreeably the busy men of the age, who only valued themselves for being in motion, and passing through a series of trifling and insignificant actions. In the heat of his discourse, seeing a piece of money lying on my table, I defy, says he, any of these active persons to produce half the adventures that this twelve-penny-piece has been engaged in, were it possible for him to give us an account of his life.

My friend's talk made so odd an impression upon my mind, that soon after I was in bed I fell insensibly into a most unaccountable *Resverie*, that had neither moral nor design in it, and cannot be so properly called a dream as a delirium.

Methoughts the shilling that lay upon the table reared itself upon its edge, and turning the face towards me, opened his mouth, and in a soft silver sound gave me the following account of his life and adventures.

I was born, says he, on the side of a mountain, near a little village of *Peru*, and made a voyage to *England* in an ingot, under the convoy of *Sir Francis Drake*. I was soon after my arrival taken out of my *Indian* habit, refined, naturalized, and put into the *British* mode, with the face of Queen *Elizabeth* on one side, and the arms of the country on the other. Being thus equipped, I found in me a wonderful inclination to ramble and visit all the parts of the new world into which I was brought. The people very much favoured my natural disposition, and shifted me so fast from hand to hand, that before I was five years old, I had travelled into almost every corner of the nation. But in the beginning of my sixth year, to my unspeakable grief, I fell into the hands of a miserable old fellow, who clapped me into an iron chest, where I found five hundred more of my own quality who lay under the same confinement. The only relief we had was to be taken out and counted over in the fresh air every morning and evening. After an imprisonment of several years, we heard some body knocking at our chest, and breaking it open with an hammer. This, we found, was the old man's heir, who, as his father lay a dying, was so good as to come to our release. He separated us that very day. What was the fate of my companions I know not: as for my self, I was sent to the apothecary's shop for a pint of sack. The apothecary gave me to an herb-woman, the herb-woman to a butcher, the butcher to a brewer, and the brewer to his wife, who made a present of me to a nonconformist preacher. After this manner I made my way merrily through the world; for, as I told you before, we shillings love nothing so much as travelling. I sometimes fetched in a shoulder of mutton, sometimes a play-book, and often had the satisfaction to treat a templer at a twelvepenny ordinary, or carry him with three friends to *Westminster hall*.

In the midst of this pleasant progress which I made from place to place, I was arrested by a superstitious old woman, who shut me up in a greazy purse in pursuance of a foolish saying, that while she kept a Queen *Elizabeth*'s shilling about her, she should never be without money. I continued here a close prisoner for many months, till at last I was exchanged for eight and forty farthings.

I thus rambled from pocket to pocket till the beginning of the Civil Wars, when, to my shame be it spoken, I was employed in raising soldiers against the King: for being of a very tempting breadth, a serjeant made use of me to inveigle country fellows, and list them in the service of the Parliament.

As soon as he had made one man sure, his way was to oblige him to take a shilling of a more homely figure, and then practise the same trick upon another. Thus I continued doing great mischief to the Crown, till my officer chancing one morning to walk abroad earlier than ordinary, sacrificed me to his pleasures, and made use of me to seduce a milk-maid. This wench bent me, and gave me to her sweetheart, applying more properly than she intended, the usual form of *To my Love and from my Love*. This ungenerous gallant marrying her within a few days after, pawned me for a dram of brandy, and drinking me out the next day, I was beaten flat with an hammer, and again set a running.

After many adventures, which it would be tedious to relate, I was sent to a young spendthrift in company with the will of his deceased father. The young fellow, who, I found, was very extravagant, gave great demonstrations of joy at the receiving the will; but opening it, he found himself disinherited, and cut off from the possession of a fair estate, by virtue of my being made a present to him. This put him into such a passion, that after having taken me in his hand and cursed me, he squirred me away from him as far as he could fling me. I chanced to light in an unfrequented place under a dead wall, where I lay undiscovered and useless during the usurpation of *Oliver Cromwell*.

About a year after the King's return, a poor cavalier that was walking there about dinner-time, fortunately cast his eye upon me, and to the great joy of us both carried me to a cook's shop, where he dined upon me, and drank the King's health. When I came again into the world, I found that I had been happier in my retirement than I thought, having probably by that means escaped wearing a monstrous pair of breeches.

Being now of great credit and antiquity, I was rather looked upon as a medal than an ordinary coin; for which reason a gambler laid hold of me, and converted me to a counter, having got together some dozens of us for that use. We led a melancholy life in his possesion, being busy at those hours wherein current coin is at rest, and partaking the fate of our master, being in a few moments valued at a crown, a pound, or a sixpence, according to the situation in which the fortune of the cards placed us. I had at length the good luck to see my master break, by which means I was again sent abroad under my primitive denomination of a shilling.

I shall pass over many other accidents of less moment, and hasten to that fatal catastrophe when I fell into the hands of an artist, who conveyed me under ground, and with an unmerciful pair of sheers cut off my titles, clipped my brims, retrench'd my shape, rubbed me to my inmost ring; and in short so spoiled and pillaged me, that he did not leave me worth a groat. You may think what a confusion I was in to see my self thus curtailed and disfigured. I should have been ashamed to have showed my head, had not all my old aquaintance been reduced to the same shameful figure, excepting some few that were punched through the belly. In the midst of this general calamity, when every body thought our misfortune irretrievable, and our case desperate, we were thrown into the furnace together, and as it often happens with cities rising out of a fire, appeared with greater beauty and lustre than we could ever boast of before. What has happened to me since this change of sex which you now see, I shall take some other opportunity to relate. In the mean time I shall only repeat two adventures as being very extraordinary, and neither of them having ever happened to me above once in my life. The first was my being in a poet's pocket, who was so taken with the brightness and novelty of my appearance, that it gave occasion to the finest burlesque poem in the *British* language, entitled from me, *The Splendid Shilling*. The second adventure, which I must not omit, happened to me in the year 1703, when I was given away in charity to a blind man; but indeed this was by a mistake, the person who gave me having heedlessly thrown me into the hat among a penniworth of farthings.

Being the fictitious history of the wanderings and adventures of a silver shilling.

'If a man is wise, he gets rich, an' if he gets rich, he gets foolish, or his wife does. That's what keeps the money moving around.'

FINLEY PETER DUNNE, OBSERVATIONS BY MR DOOLEY (1902)

PAPER MONEY

As soon as men could write, they began to replace cash with written documents. Traders and bankers in Babylon were familiar with notes and 'cheques'; the merchants of Islam in 10th-century Cairo made use of bills of exchange, promissory notes, letters of credit, bank notes and cheques; and medieval Europe had developed similar devices — particularly the bill of exchange — by the early 13th-century, with the first known endorsement in 1410.

Goldsmiths' 'promissory notes' — handed to people who deposited with them their surplus cash which began to be passed from hand to hand, became a forerunner of the 'bank note'. The bank note as we know it has existed in Sweden since 1661. After its foundation in 1694, the Bank of England wrote out 'running cash notes' (essentially bank notes); unlike modern notes, however, these early notes specified the name of the depositor and the amount deposited in the Bank, which was 'payable on demand'.

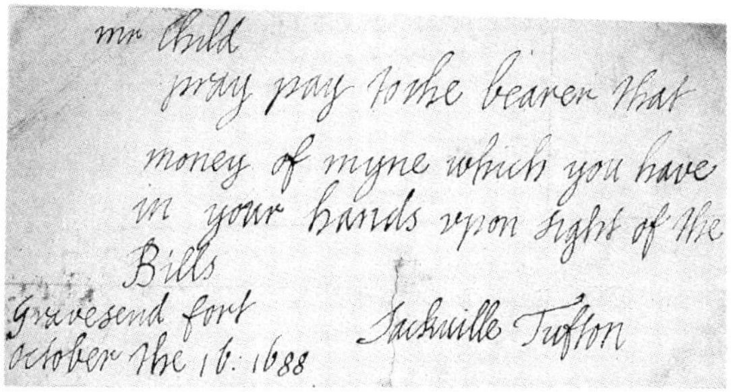
mr Child
pray pay to the bearer that
money of myne which you have
in your hands upon sight of the
Bills
Gravesend fort
October the 16: 1688
Sackville Tufton

Cheque drawn on Francis Child, 16 October, 1688

The first series of 'cheques' in England — also originating in goldsmiths' transactions — date from around 1660 and were drawn by Nicholas Vanacker on his banker William Morris.

A long and heated debate ensued as consternation grew: was a bank note money? Were cheques money? Were bank notes credit? What was money? The discussion continued for over a century.

Paper money was a further development.

David Hume, the English historian, philosopher and economist was, even in 1752, an opponent of 'this new invention of paper bank bills and chequer notes', fearing primarily that it could prove to be a licence to print money unbacked by real wealth.

Fear of paper money not being ultimately exchangeable for 'the real thing' — gold — continued for many years, and provoked numerous cartoons. In the House of Commons, Richard Brinsley Sheridan, MP, made a speech in 1797 alluding to 'an elderly lady in the city of great credit and long standing who had unfortunately fallen into bad company' . . . which was used by the cartoonist James Gillray.

There were, however, some advantages to a paper form of payment. Sebastien Mercier felt it could ease transactions, having observed how at the same period in Paris:

> **'. . . on the 10th, 20th and 30th day of the month, from ten in the morning until midday, one meets porters bent double under the burden of bags of money. They run as if an enemy army was about to surprise the city, which proves that we have not yet succeeded in creating a happy political symbol (the bank note) to replace all this metal, which should be represented by a symbol not requiring to be moved, instead of being transferred from cashbox to cashbox.'**

But gold and silver could have 'inflationary' consequences:

> 'Gold and silver are ceaselessly drawn from the bowels of the earth, are spread every year throughout Europe and increase the amount of coin there. Nations do not thereby really become more wealthy, but their wealth becomes more voluminous: the price of foodstuffs and other things necessary to life increases by turn, one has to pay more and more gold and silver to buy a loaf of bread, a house or a suit of clothes . . .'
>
> *CHARLES MATHON DE LA COUR (1788)*

Yet paper money in the form of bank notes had existed in the 9th century in both Egypt and China. Marco Polo was clearly impressed when he visited the great Kubla Khan in his city of Cambaluc at the end of the 13th-century:

> 'In this city of Cambaluc [Peking] is the mint of the grand khan who may well be said to possess the secret of the alchemists as he has the art of making money by the following process. He has the bark stripped from mulberry trees, whose leaves are used for feeding silk worms. From this is taken the thin inner rind which lies between the coarser bark and the wood of the tree. This is pounded into a pulp which is then rolled out in sheets resembling paper but quite black. When the sheets are ready for use, he has them cut into pieces of different sizes, nearly square, but somewhat longer than they are wide. Of these, the smallest pass for a half tornesel, another slightly larger for a whole tornesel. The next sizes are worth the silver half groats and groats of Venice. Larger pieces still are valued at two, five and ten groats; others again at one, two, three and even up to ten bezants of gold. All this paper money is issued with as much form and ceremony as if it were actually of pure gold or silver; for to each note a number of specially appointed officers subscribe their names and affix their signets. When this has been duly done, the principal officer deputed by the Great Khan dips into vermilion the royal seal committed to his custody and stamps with it the piece of paper, so that the form of the seal tinged with vermilion remains impressed upon it.

Thereby it receives full authenticity as current money and the act of counterfeiting it is punished with death. The Grand Khan has made year after year so much of this money (which costs him nothing) that he could buy with it all the coin in the world. All his payments are made with these paper notes which circulate in all the kingdoms and provinces over which his rule extends. No-one dares to refuse it in payment on pain of death. Nay all men accept it readily; for wherever they go, they can buy with it whatever they want – gold, silver, precious stones and wares of all kinds. Moreover, ten bezants' worth of paper money weighs less than one golden bezant.

When anyone possesses paper money which from long use has become damaged, he can take it to the Mint; and there, upon payment of only three percent, he will receive new notes in exchange. Moreover, anyone desirous of procuring gold or silver for manufacturing purposes may in like manner apply to the Mint and can there obtain by paper money payments the bullion he requires. All the Khan's armies are paid with this currency, which serves the soldiers as well as gold or silver.

Now you have heard how and why the Grand Khan possesses a greater mount of treasure than anyone in the world.'

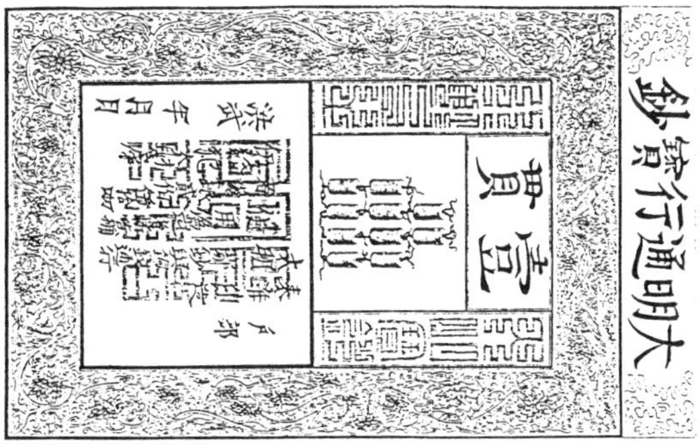

A somewhat later — 1380 — Chinese bank note.

While Marco Polo was admiring the Great Khan's ingenious scheme, several of his countrymen were establishing the basis of modern banking throughout Europe.

The first references to banking and money-changing are in Genoese notarial records of the 12th and 13th centuries. So-called bankers and money-changers were:

> **'. . . forming partnerships, accepting time and demand deposits, extending credit to customers, and even participating directly in business ventures beyond the seas.'**

Time deposits yielded returns. In a contract dated 9 December 1190:

> **'. . . a certain Bernardus bancherius promised to pay 10 per cent a year on an amount of £11, Genoese currency, deposited with his 'bank', and repayable on eight days' notice.'**

And the chronicler and diplomat Philippe de Commines placed a time deposit with the Medici bank which, instead of yielding a fixed percentage:

> **'. . . entitled him to participate in the profits, at the discretion of the bank.'**

By the following century money-changers were an important link between Mints and the public, and were operating more like banks, providing an important financial service for merchants.

> **'. . . it was customary for merchants to have bank accounts and to use them in order to make payments of transfer. Not infrequently, depositors were granted credit by being allowed to overdraw their accounts. Finally, there existed inter-bank arrangements which permitted payments by transfer even if the debtor and creditor kept their bank accounts with different money-changers . . .'**

The ledgers of the Bruges money-changers prove that they all had clearing accounts with one another .

The money-changers operated on a fractional reserve principle. According to the books of the Bruges money-changer Guillame Ruyelle, he had a cash reserve of about 30 per cent of his deposits. Besides allowing overdrafts they invested some of their resources directly in business ventures, a dangerous practice which largely explains the high death rate of the medieval banks.

However, in the field of 'international banking' it was the merchants who extended their trading activities to regulate their foreign credit transactions, acquire balances abroad and introduce the precursor of the bill of exchange.

A regular 'money market' was in the process of being created. Merchants' manuals and accounts give quite detailed information on exchange quotations and seasonal variations, usance, parities, brokerage, book transfers as well as transfer of funds, bills of exchange and arbitrage, and letters of credit to travellers and pilgrims.

Exchange rates and their uncertain fluctuations created a basis for 'interest' charges, thereby avoiding accusations of 'usury'.

Cheques, or written orders of payment, were first used in the 14th century whenever a customer was unable to be present at a transfer — which until that time was done in the presence of both the creditor and debtor. Oral orders carried more weight initially than the written order, but the latter became popular in Amsterdam by the 17th century, though not until a century later in Venice.

A complex European merchant banking network had thus grown up by the mid-14th century, with bank branches and correspondents in the major cities. And the problems it encountered were no different to those encountered in the 20th century, including the collapse of three major banks — the Acciaiuoli, the Peruzzi and the Bardi. All three had over-extended their credit — to King Edward III of England, to finance his wars, and to the King of Naples.

The end of the 14th century saw the rise of the richest merchant banker of the period, Francesco Datini, with his headquarters in Prato (Tuscany) and branches in Florence, Pisa, Avignon, Barcelona, Valencia and Palma di Mallorca.

His papers and accounts have survived, and give us a very clear and colourful picture of banking in that period.

A typical bill of exchange:

> **'In the name of God, the 12th of February 1395. Pay at usance*, by this first of exchange, to Giovanni Asopardo £306.13s.4d Barcelonesi, which are for 400 florins received here from Bartolomeo Agarzoni, at 15s.4d per florin. Pay and charge to our account there and reply. God keep you. Francesco and Andrea, greetings from Genoa**
> **Accepted March 13.'**

**usance was the time customarily allowed for the payment of a bill of exchange. The usance between Genoa and Barcelona was 20 days.*

An extract from *The Merchant of Prato* gives some idea of the scale and complexity of his operations:

> **'Francesco's correspondents in Bruges often used their credit balances with his branch in Barcelona to make remittances to Italy, and vice versa. For instance, in a letter dated 9 January 1400 we find the Orlandini firm of Bruges instructing Datini's branch in Barcelona to remit 1,000 florins to Genoa, 1,000 ducats to Venice, and 1,000 florins to Florence, covering these transactions by drawing on Bruges. And on 21 February of the same year, the firm Bernardo degli Alberti of Venice drew a bill of 400 ducats at 16s.8d Barcelonesi per ducat on the Datini branch in Barcelona, requesting them to charge the amount — £333.6s.8d Barcelonesi — to the Alberti Co. of Bruges.**
>
> **. . . The bank offered its clients a variety of services: acceptance and issue of bills of exchange, loans (though only to other trading companies or private clients, not to princes, Popes or Communes), endorsements (avalli), guarantees (fideiussioni), and correspondence accounts in one or more currencies. For payments to third parties cheques, which were only just coming into use, were freely accepted.'**

In the counting house, Van Reymerswael.

Like most bankers of his time, Datini was involved in earning interest on his money, but was wary of patently usurious exchanges. His pragmatic partner in Valencia warned him in a letter of 30 January 1394:

> 'I think you have already heard from our men in Genoa that the King (of Aragon) has brought the usurers (some Italian merchants) to trial, and has had leave from the Pope to do so. They consider those who sell with deferred payment to be usurers, and if they intend to follow this rule, they will ruin this city.'

His partner in Barcelona, however, caused him some problems. In 1406 he wrote to him:

> 'If you feel inclined to buy or sell money on the exchange, and attend to the business of many money-changers . . . find someone who is capable of doing it, for I will not be involved to satisfy your greed, nor dwell in constant fear.'

IRIS ORIGO, THE MERCHANT OF PRATO, 1957

CHAPTER 2

— ILLICIT MONEY —

'He who practiceth usury goes to hell, and he who practiceth it not tendeth to destitution.'

BENVENUTO DA IMOLA, EARLY 14th CENTURY

We acquire money by licit or 'illicit' means. The 'illicit' money acquired either not through our own hard work, or through misplaced hard work — such as in forgery — has always evoked disapproval, disdain . . . and not a little envy.

The medieval definition of usury involved a 'certain' profit on a loan, no matter what the size of that profit. So, to avoid condemnation by both Church and State of usurious practice — a serious affair which threatened those participating in it with eternal damnation — uncertainty and risk had to be built into any such financial transaction. Two ways presented themselves: incorporating a foreign exchange transaction in any such deal or borrowing; or offering the lender a part-ownership in the undertaking for which he had provided money, and repaying him later with his due share of the enterprise.

By the early 14th century not only usurers but all those who authorised or protected usurers were threatened with excommunication.

Usury practised by the Jews, however, was tolerated. As they already had no hope of salvation because of their essential lack of faith, the Church did not need to concern itself with their souls. Moreover, they were, by their actions, saving Christians from being tempted into such damnable practices; and they increased the coffers of the State, for they were taxed on their usurious proceeds.

In a further twist, Jews in 15th-century Germany themselves provided a sound justification for their usury: if the Torah and its understanding was better disseminated throughout the country — which was their ambition — this was because they earned a living from their money trade; thus, not needing to work, they could devote more time to studying the Torah.

"UNDER THE ROSE."

However, even clerics recognised that there had to be some incentive to persuade people to part with their money. St Thomas Aquinas, the 13th-century theologian, recognised the legitimacy of 'damnum emergens' — compensation for a loss which the lender would suffer if the borrower failed to repay money within

the stipulated time. He distinguished it clearly from the illegitimate 'lucrum cessans' — loss of potential gain, ie, what the lender might have earned had he not lent to this particular person and put the money to other use — saying: 'why should not your gains cease, in ethics, during this time when you yourself were taking no trouble to work for it'.

For this was the essence. The main accusation levelled by the medieval Church — and hence the State — against usurers was that they sold 'time', which belonged to God alone.

'The usurer wants to make a profit without any work at all and even while sleeping, which is against the teaching of the Lord: 'You will earn your bread by the sweat of your brow.''

THOMAS OF CHOBHAM, 12th CENTURY

Worse still, the usurer made his money work for him; even peasants allowed their animals rest on Sundays and feast days; the usurer — whose money was his 'cattle' — did not even respect the day of rest.

Such condemnation did not stop usurers from practising their trade. But it did affect their spiritual life, and raised the question of whether they would be forever damned, to spend eternity in Hell, or could expect salvation. And resolving this issue was crucial to the development of commercial capitalism as practised by merchant bankers in medieval Europe.

The Church held that there were two detestable kinds of avarice subject to trial and punishment: usury and simony. Those who practised either would die horrible deaths, 'opening the dance of the damned' with their habitual companions — Satan and demons. Some usurers, of course, expressed penitence on their deathbeds. But Heaven for such men was unthinkable.

At the end of the 12th century the Church resolved its dilemma: purgatory was 'invented' — the interim stage between Heaven and Hell where these 'robbers of time' would await the Day of Judgement.

SEBASTIAN BRANT, SHIP OF FOOLS (15th CENTURY)

'The usurers are vile and rash,
The man of poverty they thrash,
They'd care not if the world should crash . . .
We'd punish him for all his tricks
From him we must remove the ticks
And pluck his pinions with elation
Who buys up goods on speculation,
The wine and corn in all the land,
No sin, dishonor stays his hand,
So that a poor man cannot flee
Starvation with his family.
Thus prices mount, it must be clear,
They're higher now than those last year,
If wine now costs a scant ten pound
Next month 'twill certainly be found
You'll pay full thirty when you buy.
The same is true of wheat, spelt, rye.
The great abuse need not be stressed
Of money, kind and interest
Of loans, pawn business oft unsound:
In one day some will earn a pound
More profit than a year should hold,
They lend in silver, ask for gold,
You borrow ten, elevn's due,
They're more usurious than the Jew.
Their business now the Jews may lose
For it is done by Christian Jews.'

'A certaine usurer of Mentz, drawing near unto his Death, bound his Friendes by oath, that in his grave they should put a purse full of Money, under his head; which [was] done accordingly. His sepulcher [being] afterwards opened, that it might bee taken out, there was seen a Divell powring melting golde downe his throat with a ladle.'

A PLEA AGAINST USURY . . .

A discourse upon usury (1572) addressed to 'the right honourable hyghe and myghte Earl, hys most especial and singuler deere Lord, the Lord Robert Duddeley, Erle of Leycester, Baron of Denbigh, master of the horse to the Quene's Maiestie' (etc) . . . by Dr Thomas Wilson, one time Member of Parliament and ambassador to the Netherlands:

> '. . . thys I reache at, that where amongst a number of gawles and great greefes in thys common weale there spredeth one especial mischiefe as yll, nay woorse than anye plague, my meaning is to sett all other faultes aparte, and to disclose this one above the rest unto your Lordship, that by your honorable meanes and great aucthoritye it maye at the leaste bee somewhat refourmed, yf not altogether amended or taken away. I do meane that ouglie, detestable and hurtefull synne of usurie, whiche, being but one in grossenes of name, caries many a mischief linked into it in nature, the same synne being nowe so rancke througout all Englande, not in London onelye, that men have altogether forgotten free lending, and have geven themselvees wholye to lyve by fowle gayning, makinge the lone of monye a kinde of merchandise, a thinge directlye against all lawe, against nature, and against god. And what should this meane, that, in steade of charitable dealing and the use of almose (for lending is a spice therof) hardenes of harte hath nowe gotten place, and greedie gayne is cheefelye folowed and horrible extorcion commonly used? I do verely beleve, the ende of thys worlde is nyghe at hande.
>
> And the more is thys evill to bee pitied, because men doe lulle themselves with the exercise thereof in such sorte as thoughe there were none offenses in it at all, whereas amongst all offenses next to Idolatrie, and the renouncing of god and hys magistrates upon earth, there is none more heynous, none more offensive, and none more hurtfull to anye well governed common weale. For besides that the very sinne of usurie is expresslie forbidden by godds worde, aswel as either thefte, aduolotrie, or whoredome, the countrey and realme where thys

offence is commonlie used cannot longe continue in prosperous wellfare. And sorie I am to saye it, but I see it and knowe it overwel, and therefore I must needes saie it: I do not knowe anye place in christendome so muche subiect to thys foule synne of usurie as the whole realme of Englande ys at thys present, and hathe bene of late yeares. For men of wealth are nowe wholy geeven every wheare all together to idleness, to gett their gaine with ease, and to lyve by lending upon the onely sweate and labour of others. Whereas god willeth everye man to lyve in hys vocation, and hee that will not laboure eyther with body or minde according to his callyng rightly should not eate at al, forbidding men to make lending a kinde of living. But these men do not live in any vocation, but beinge the diuels knownen apprentices in earth, and bound to doe as hee woulde have them, seeke when they are dead to serve hym in hell, as I take it. For god sayeth by hys prophete David, that (Psal. 115) he shall never dwell in hys tabernacle, that hathe put out hys mony for usury. And therefore whether should suche men looke to goe, when they are deade, but straighte to the divell, seeynge in earth they serve such a master?'

Punishment of usurers in Hell.

. . . AND A PLEA FOR IT

According to the 18th-century liberal philosopher Jeremy Bentham, there was, however, another point of view:

> 'Among the various species of modifications of liberty, of which on different occasions we have heard so much in England, I do not recollect ever seeing anything yet offered in [sic] behalf of the liberty of making one's own terms in money bargains. From so general and universal a neglect, it is an old notion of mine, as you well know, that this meek and unassuming species of liberty has been suffering much injustice.
>
> A fancy has taken me, just now, to trouble you with my reasons . . . In a word, the proposition I have been accustomed to lay down to myself on this subject is the following one, viz. that no man of ripe years and of sound mind, acting freely, and with his eyes open, ought to be hindered, with a view to his advantage, from making such bargain, in the way of obtaining money, as he thinks fit: nor (what is a necessary consequence) anybody hindered from supplying him, upon any terms he thinks proper to accede to.
>
> This proposition, were it to be received, would level, you see, at one stroke, all the barriers which law, either statute or common, have in their united wisdom set up, either against the sin of Usury, or against the hard-named and little-heard-of-practice of Champetry.
>
> On this occasion, were it any individual antagonist I had to deal with, my part would be a smooth and easy one. 'You, who fetter contracts; you who lay restraints on the liberty of man, it is for you' (I should say) 'to assign a reason for your doing so.''

JEREMY BENTHAM, DEFENCE OF USURY, SHEWING THE IMPOLICY OF THE PRESENT LEGAL RESTRAINTS ON THE TERMS OF PECUNIARY BARGAINS (1787)

FORGERY . . . AND DEBASEMENT

A crime . . . maybe . . . and usually severely punished. But the Chinese practised this art to such a high level of perfection that when the government reorganised their coinage in 116 BC, 'the most notorious and skilful of the forgers were enlisted in the service of the state and given official positions in the mint.'

Romans, by contrast, condemned counterfeiters to the mines, or to be crucified. This may be why those involved in this nefarious process in London around 200 AD hurriedly dumped 100 ceramic coin moulds used for making such denarii (from which came the old 'd' penny sign) into a local rubbish tip — which was unearthed in the City in 1988.

And the Anglo-Saxon Chronicle recounts simply and chillingly how, in 1125 in Winchester, there were assembled all the 'moneyers' (forgers), and:

> **'. . . when they came thither, they were then taken one by one and each deprived of the right hand and the testicles below. All this was done in twelve days.'**

Debasement was a common problem in most societies. The Romans knew it well, and the Emperor Nero practised it formally, substituting silver with an alloy. Others followed his example to help them obtain revenue by lowering the content of gold or silver, by lowering the weight, or by paring or cutting off pieces (clipping).

For a brief period at the end of the 17th century in England, 'pots, pans, door knockers and pieces of ordnance' were assembled at the Mint and used to create coins — creating a situation where a mortgage for a thousand pounds was cleared off — as Macaulay put it — by a bag of counters made out of old kettles. For a similar 'fraud' on his subjects some 400 years earlier, Philip the Fair of France was threatened with excommunication by the Pope.

The introduction of round coins — a technological innovation produced by a mill worked by horses in the Tower Mint — was a step in the direction of preventing clipping and shearing, as were the savage laws against coining and clipping. As the historian T. B. Macaulay recounts:

> **'Hurdles, with four, five, six wretches convicted of counterfeiting or mutilating the money of the realm were dragged month after month up Holborn Hill. One morning seven men were hanged and one woman burned for clipping.'**

Skulls impaled on London Bridge.

(LONDON GAZETTE, 1847)

'. . . counterfeiting seems to have reached its maximum in the reign of Queen Elizabeth, for when that princess called in the base money by proclamation, in order to have it converted into sterling coin, at a separate mint in the Tower, it was found that, out of 631,950 pounds of current currency, there was 387,531 pounds of dross.

The Antiquaries Agarde and Hearne relate a similar anecdote connected with this purification of the coin, which, if true, gives cause to suspect that it had been fluxed with arsenic. They state that many of the workmen employed in melting the base coins 'feel sick to death with the savour, and that they were advised to drink in a dead man's skull for their rescue. Accordingly a warrant was procured from the Council to take off the heads from London Bridge, and to make cups of them out of which they drank, and found some relief, although most of them died.''

But sometimes the gains seemed worth the risk, and one clipper was able to offer £6,000 for a pardon. It was rejected, but:

'. . . the fame of his riches did much to counteract the effect which the spectacle of his death was designed to produce. Nay the severity of the punishment gave encouragement to the crime. For the practice of clipping, pernicious as it was, did not excite in the common mind a detestation resembling that with which men regard murder, arson, robbery or even theft. The injury done by a whole body of clippers to the whole society was indeed immense: but each particular act of clipping was a trifle. To pass a half-crown after paring a pennyworth of silver from it seemed a minute, almost imperceptible fault.'

'Bad money drives good money out of circulation.'

GRESHAM'S LAW

A suspicious coin — possibly clipped, and of less value than its 'face value'. Tradesmen in the 17th and 18th century were particularly wary of such coins.

However, clipping and debasement caused real hardships:

> 'Nothing could be purchased without a dispute. Over every counter there was a wrangling from morning till night. The workman and his employer had a quarrel as regularly as the Saturday came round. On a fair day or a market day, the clamours, the reproaches, the taunts, the curses were incessant: and it was well if no booth was overturned and no heads broken. No merchant could contract to deliver goods without making some stipulation about the quality of the coin in which he was to be paid. Even men of business were often bewildered

by the confusion into which all pecuniary transactions were thrown. The simple and the careless were pillaged without mercy by extortioners whose demands grew even more rapidly than the money shrank. The cost of necessities of life rose fast . . . the labourer found that the bit of metal, which when he received it, was called a shilling would hardly, when he wanted to purchase a pot of beer or loaf of bread, go as far as sixpence.'

Even the renowned 17th-century poet Dryden was put in the position of accepting forty brass shillings and a parcel of clipped money as payment from his highly successful publisher, Tonson. On another occasion Dryden returned Tonson's money and demanded guineas at twenty-nine shillings apiece. He complained: 'I lost 30 shillings or more by the last payment of 50 pounds.'

William Guest, executed at Tyburn on 14 October 1767, for high treason in diminishing the current coin of the realm, was a clerk at the Bank of England:

'This man's crime was aggravated by a breach of public trust. He was the son of a clergyman of unblemished character, of the city of Worcester, who placed him apprentice to a genteel business.

He then came to London and took a shop in Holborn, where he carried on business for some years, with the usual success of trade. His father's good name assisted him in procuring a clerkship in the Bank of England, and there the constant handling of gold shook his integrity.

He took a house in Broad Street Buildings, in a room in the upper part of which he used to work. Having procured a curious machine for milling guineas, not unlike a machine made use of by mathematical-instrument makers, he used to take guineas from his drawer at the bank, file them and then return them to the bank, and take guineas of full weight in their stead. Of their filings he made ingots, which he sold to an assayer, who, on his trial, deposed that the filings were of the same standard as our guineas.

The cashier of the bank, having his suspicions aroused, sent

Mr Sewallis and Mr Humberton, servants of the bank, with proper officers to search Mr Guest's house in Broad Street Buildings. In a room up two pair of stairs there stood a mahogany nest of drawers, in which on being broken open were found a vice, files and an instrument proper for milling the edges of guineas. Mr Throughton, a jeweller, deposed he had sold two bars of gold for the prisoner, one of which weighed forty-six and the other forty-eight ounces.

The circumstances above mentioned were deemed to adduce such evidence of guilt that the jury did not hesitate to convict Mr Guest: the consequence of which was that sentence of death was passed on him.

After conviction this malefactor made the most serious preparations for the awful change that awaited him. Consistent with the plan respecting persons convicted of high treason, he was conveyed to the place of execution on a sledge. His dress consisted of a suit of mourning and a club wig. At Tyburn, the place of execution, he appeared to exhibit every mark of penitence and resignation. He prayed devoutly, and when he was turned off, and his body had hung the accustomed time, it was delivered to his friends to be buried.'

(THE COMPLETE NEWGATE CALENDAR)

In the early 19th century in England, execution — or possibly banishment — were still the routine punishments for creating — and worst, for handling — forged notes.

'Between 1808-11, numberless impositions were practised upon the unwary in the metropolis in passing notes manufactured in imitation of the notes of the Bank of England. These were traced to have first originated in the Fleet Prison, a receptacle for debtors only. These notes were printed on paper similar to that used by the Bank of England; but upon the slightest inspection they were easily detected; which creates surprise at so many being imposed upon. The great success of sharpers passing them chiefly arose from the hurry of business of those imposed upon, and from the novelty of the fraud. The shop keeper would see the word one, two, three, etc, an exact imitation, but did not examine further, or he would have found that instead of 'pounds' the counterfeit expressed 'pence'; and this, with all the wisdom of our laws, was found not to be forgery. Instead of 'Governor and Company of the Bank of England' the worthless paper substituted 'Governor and Company of the Bank of Fleet'. Such gross deception we may be sure could not long be practised and every tradesman who had dearly been taught precaution, on taking a bank-note convinced himself that it was not a 'Fleet'.'

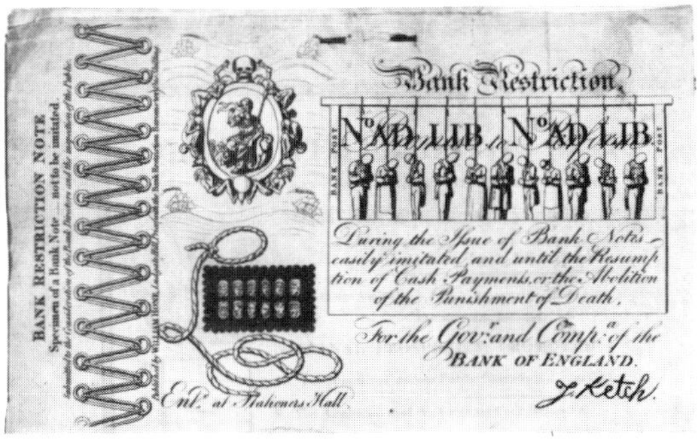

After seeing a woman hanged outside Newgate Prison in 1819 – merely for passing a forged note, George Cruikshank drew this note, signed by J. Ketch, the common nickname for a hangman.

The circulation of 'Fleet notes' was generally entrusted to profligate women, who cohabited with the men who made them.

(THE COMPLETE NEWGATE CALENDAR)

CHAPTER 3

—TEMPLES TO MONEY... AND THOSE WHO SERVE THEM—

'Bankers are like everyone else, except richer.'

OGDEN NASH

The Square Mile has always been home to financial institutions. From the early days of Thomas Gresham's Royal Exchange, of Chepeside and Lombard Street 'where the Italians gathered', and the coffee houses, who you met in its alleyways was at the hub of what news and information you had and how you used it.

The 'City' — which even in Edwardian days had fewer than 400,000 people working in its 40,000 firms — remained an exclusive club until the 1970s, when 'foreigners' and technology intruded.

In the inter-war years, one writer explained one of the 'essential qualities of the City':

> '. . . the sweet sellers from their surrounding nooks and crannies, the newspaper boys, the hot chestnut man in winter, Mr Douch our chemist in Throgmorton Street who dispensed enormous glasses of fizzy, flowing restoratives for thick heads — knew one another.'

Some twenty years ago the still leisurely pace of the City struck one writer:

> '. . . in the narrow streets and lanes of a small area, people are able to walk between any bank, insurance company, stockbroker or commodity trader on foot. The top-hatted gentlemen of Lombard Street, the money market proper, stroll around every one of the banks — British, American or foreign — every morning to scoop up the excess money and sell or buy bills. Almost every country in the world is represented by branches of banks and business firms, and their managers enter into the business life of the City as full and equal members.'

THE AMBASSADOR, 1966

'The Bank'

Walter de Zoete, the Edwardian stockbroker, would undoubtedly have been horrified at this leisurely pace: 'In the City', he told his son, 'as a young man you never walk but always run.'

Keeping up with old traditions, he also refused to use that new-fangled contraption, the telephone . . . banishing it to the basement.

Keeping up with other old traditions, the Stock Exchange refused to allow 'strangers' into their halls even when it became an issue to be dealt with by a Royal Commission in 1878. The doors were finally opened in 1953. Those other 'strangers' — women — were not allowed in until 1973.

Old fears also die hard. A novice clerk on joining Rothschilds about 100 years ago was convinced by his colleagues that circumcision was a *sine qua non* for acceptance and advancement. Overcome with gratitude, however, when they then informed him that the Board had decided to make an exception in his case, he went personally to thank the chairman — to the latter's great mirth.

'In the yeare 1570 on the 23 of Ianuarie, the Queenes Maiestie, attended with her Nobilitie, came from her house at the Strand called Sommerset house, and entered the citie by Temple Barre, through Fleetstreete, Cheape, and so by the North side of the Bursse through threeneedle streete, to Sir Thomas Greshams house in Bishopsgate streete, where she dined. After dinner, her Maiestie returning through Cornehill, entered the Bursse on the southside, and after that she had viewed every part therof above the ground, especially the Pawne*, which was richly furnished with all sorts of the finest wares in the Citie: shee caused the same Bursse by an Herald and a Trumpet, to be proclaimed the Royal Exchange, and so to be called from thenceforth, and not otherwise.'

JOHN STOW, SURVEY OF LONDON (1603)

Corrupted from 'bahn', German for path or walk.

GRESHAM'S EXCHANGE

'The merchants of the exchange are generally men of good habit; their words are generally better than their consciences; their discourse ordinarily begins in water, but ends in wine. The frequenting the walks twice a day, and a careless laughter, argues they are sound; if they visit not once a day, 'tis suspected they are cracking or broken. Their countenance is ordinarily shaped by their successes at sea, either merry, sad or desperate . . .'

DESCRIPTION OF THE MERCHANTS OF THE EXCHANGE (1632)

'The new Bourse, Flemish in character, was a long, four-storeyed building with a huge double balcony. A bell-tower, crowned by a huge grasshopper, stood on one side of the chief entrance. The bell in this tower summoned the merchants to the spot at 12 noon and 6 in the evening . . .

Each corner of the building, and the peak of every dormer window, was crowned with a grasshopper. Within Gresham's Bourse were piazzas for wet weather, and the covered walkways were adorned with statues of English kings. A statue of Gresham stood near the north end of the western piazza. At the Great Fire of 1666 this statue alone remained there uninjured . . .

The piazzas were supported by marble pillars, and above were 100 small shops . . .

Many of the shops of the Bourse remained unlet until Queen Elizabeth's visit in 1570, which gave them a lustre which tended to make them fashionable. Gresham, anxious to have the Bourse worthy of such a visitor, went round twice in one day to all the shopkeepers in the 'upper pawn' and offered them all the shops they would furnish and light up with wax rent-free for a whole year . . . There were also sellers of armour, apothecaries, booksellers, goldsmiths and glass-sellers.

The shops soon grew rich and more fashionable . . . but the

vulgar opinion of Gresham's wealth had him portrayed in a contemporary play as crushing a priceless pearl into a wine cup, and drinking the Queen's health.

The new exchange, like the nave of St. Paul's, soon became a resort for idlers . . . On Sundays and holidays great numbers of boys, children and 'young rogues' met there, and shouted and halloaed, so that honest citizens could not walk there for their recreation, and the parishioners of St. Bartholemew could not hear the sermon. In 1590 we find certain women prosecuted for selling apples and oranges at the Exchange gate in Cornhill, and 'amusing themselves in cursing and swearing, to the great annoyance and grief of the inhabitants and passers-by'.

In 1592 a tavern keeper who had vaults under the Exchange was fined for allowing tippling, and for broiling herrings, sprats and bacon, to the vexation of the worshipful merchants resorting to the exchange . . . In 1622 complaints were made of the rat-catchers, and sellers of dogs, birds, plants etc who hung about the south gate, especially at exchange time.

. . . great precautions were taken against fire. Feather-makers were forbidden to keep pans of fire in their shops. Some care was also taken to maintain honesty among shopkeepers, for they were forbidden to use blinds on their windows, which might obscure the shops, or throw false light on the articles vended.'

WALTER THORNBURY, OLD AND NEW LONDON (1897)

Folklore has it that a grasshopper saved the life of the young Thomas Gresham as he lay, poor and hungry, in a field. A passer-by was attracted to the spot by the chirping of a grasshopper, and so saved Thomas's life. Remembering the grasshopper, Sir Thomas later incorporated it into the Gresham crest, and used it as the symbol of the Exchange — still to be seen on the present LIFFE 19th-century building.

Over a century later, the Exchange — on its new site — still held its fascination for the writer Richard Addison, as it continued to be the meeting point for merchants from the four corners of the world.

> 'There is no place in the town which I so much love to frequent as the Royal Exchange. It gives me secret satisfaction and in some measure gratifies my vanity, as I am an Englishman, to see so rich an assembly of countrymen and foreigners consulting together upon the private business of mankind, and making this metropolis a kind of emporium for the whole earth . . . I have often been pleased to hear disputes adjusted between an inhabitant of Japan and an alderman of London; or to see a subject of the Great Mogul entering into a league with one of the Czar of Muscovy. I am infinitely delighted in mixing with these several ministers of commerce, as they are distinguished by different walks and different languages. Sometimes I am jostled among a body of Armenians; sometimes I am lost in a crowd of Jews; and sometimes make one in a group of Dutchmen. I am a Dane, Swede or Frenchman at different times; or rather fancy myself like an old philosopher who, upon being asked what countryman he was, replied he was a citizen of the world . . .'

RICHARD ADDISON, THE SPECTATOR, No. 69 (1711)

Stockjobbers, Rowlandson.

Change Alley was the meeting place for merchants, seafaring men and traders — and later for brokers dealing with the buying and selling of stocks. They met and did business in the great coffee houses of the day: Jonathan's and Garraway's. It was also the stage for the South Sea Bubble of 1720.

'The centre of the jobbing is in the kingdom of Change Alley. You may go over its limits in about a minute and a half. Stepping out of Jonathan's into the Alley, you turn your face full south; moving on a few paces and then turning to the east, you advance to Garraway's; from thence going out at the other door, you go on still east into Birchin Lane, and then halting at the Swordblade Bank, you immediately face to the north, enter Cornhill, visit two or three petty provinces on your way to the west; and thus having boxed your compass, and sailed around the stock jobbing globe, you turn into Jonathan's again.'

THE ANATOMY OF EXCHANGE ALLEY (1719)

'OPEN OUTCRY' . . . OR BUSINESS AS USUAL

The *Bank Mirror* described the atmosphere on the Stock Exchange, *c.*1795.

'The scene opens about 12, with the call of the prices of stock, the shouting out of names, the recital of news, etc, much in the following manner:

A mail come in . . . — What news? what news? — steady, steady — Consols for tomorrow — Here, Consols — You old timber-toe, have you got any scrip? — Private advices from . . . — A wicked old peer in disguise sold . . . — What do you do? — Here, Consols! Consols! — Letters from . . . — A great house has stopt — Payment of the five per cents commences — Across the Rhine . . . — The Austrians routed . . . — The French pursuing . . . — Four per cents for the opening — Four per cents — Sir Sydney Smith exchanged for . . . — Short annuities — shorts, shorts, shorts — A messenger extraordinary sent to . . . — Gibraltar fortifying against . . . — A Spanish fleet seen in . . . — The Cape of Good Hope retaken by . . . — Lottery tickets — Here, tickets, tickets, tickets — The Archduke Charles of Austria fled into . . . — India stock — Clear the way, there, Moses — Reduced, reduced — (rattles spring) — What a d..d noise you make there with the rattles — Five per cents — I'm a seller — Five per cents, five per cents — Smoke the old girl in silk shoes there! Madam do you want a broker? — Four per cents — The Dutch fleet skulked into . . . — Short annuities — The French army retreating . . . — The Austrians pursuing . . . — Consols, Consols, Bravo! — Who's afraid — Up they go, up they go — The Empress of Russia dead! — You, Levi, you're a thief, and I'm not a gentleman — Step to Garraway's and bid Isaacs come here — Bank stock — Consols — Noble news, great news — Here, Consols — St. Lucia taken . . . — St. Vincent taken . . . — French fleets blocked up. English fleets triumphant. Bravo! Up we go, up, up, up — Imperial annuities, Imperial, Imperial — Get out of my sunshine, Moses, you d..d little Israelite — Consols, Consols . . . '

'The human species, according to the best theory I can form, is composed of two distinct races — the men who borrow and the men who lend.'

CHARLES LAMB, 19th CENTURY

'To be a good banker requires some intellectual and some moral qualifications. A banker need not be a man of talent, but he should be a man of wisdom . . . a banker need not be a poet or a philosopher, a man of science or of literature, an orator or statesman . . . It is only necessary that he should possess a large portion of that practical quality which is called commonsense.'

GILBART, PRACTICAL TREATISE ON BANKING (19th CENTURY)

'The distinctive function of the banker begins as soon as he uses the money of others; as long as he uses his own money, he is only a capitalist.'

DAVID RICARDO, 18th CENTURY

'Leading financiers, being unable to follow an argument, never admit the feasibility of anything until it has been demonstrated to them by practical experience.'

JOHN MAYNARD KEYNES (20th CENTURY)

'A great business is seldom, if ever built up except on lines of the strictest integrity. A reputation for 'cuteness' and sharp dealing is fatal in great affairs . . .
This does not, of course, apply to the speculative clan. An entirely different atmosphere pervades that world. Men are only gamblers there. Stock gambling and honourable business are incompatible.'

ANDREW CARNEGIE, LATE 19th CENTURY

MIRTH IN THE HOUSE: THROWING THE TAPE.

DRAWN BY OUR SPECIAL ARTIST, S. BEGG, FROM A SKETCH BY A MEMBER OF THE HOUSE.

A GAME FOR SLACK DAYS IN THE STOCK EXCHANGE: THROWING THE TAPE OVER THE HAND-RAIL.

BANK OF ENGLAND

An island fortress — yet twice at least found to be vulnerable.

In June 1780, a mob which had assembled at Westminster to protest about the easing of restrictions on Roman Catholics, moved eastwards. After burning down Newgate prison, they set off for the Bank of England.

A force of horse and foot guards was sent to defend the building, supplemented by a band of citizen volunteers, headed by John Wilkes. Thereafter, a military force was stationed nightly within the Bank, and dinner was provided for the officer on guard and two friends. On the evening of 14 April 1793, two such gentlemen refused to leave, 'used indecent and abusive language, and slept all night at the Bank, after breaking bottles and glasses, and fighting together with the officer of the Bank yard'.

The daily march of the King's guard through the crowded streets of the Strand, Fleet Street and Cheapside caused great annoyance, as soldiers marched two abreast and jostled everyone in their way. Following a complaint, they marched in single file but not before one of their number had bayoneted a Mr Crespigny.

Arrival of Californian gold and Mexican dollars at the Bank of England.

While business went on as usual above ground, below ground things were stirring.

In 1836, the directors received an anonymous letter, stating that the writer had the means of access to their bullion room. Treating the matter as a hoax, they took no action; a second, more urgent and specific letter also failed to rouse them. It was not until the writer offered to meet them in the bullion room at any hour they pleased to name that they took the matter seriously.

Agreeing to meet the writer at a 'dark and midnight hour', a deputation from the Board, lanterns in hand, went to the bullion room and awaited their correspondent. At the appointed hour, some floorboards were removed, and a figure emerged from below. His story was simple. He had discovered the existence of an old drain beneath the room . . . and could have helped himself to vast sums of money. Instead, however, he decided to alert the bank. The directors repaid the man's honesty — for no money had been stolen — with a present of £800.

The 'open and unobstructed sewer leading directly from the gold vaults to Dowgate' was pointed out to the Building committee, and the necessary precautions taken.

THE LIVELIEST PLACE OF BUSINESS IN THE WORLD:

"RAGGING" SCENES IN THE STOCK EXCHANGE.

The obsessive behaviour which grips financiers . . . who talk, eat, breathe and sleep finance . . . is infectious.

With that well-known phrase: 'If it moves, trade it.' they literally trade anything, alive and even dead, from hogs and pork bellies to currencies and mortgages.

One broker who entered the speculative hog market in the US in the 1870s — after visiting a small town on the Mississippi, seeing nothing but hogs, everywhere, and realising that here was potential — described how:

> **'. . . for the next two weeks we sought the fellowship of pork men. Pork on the brain. We thought pork, talked pork, handled pork, dreamed of pork and did everything with it except eat it, because it cost too much . . .'**

To his relief, he found:

> **'The pork men are very much after the pattern of the Wall Street men. Jolly boys, astonished at nothing, much given to eating and drinking of good things, fond of jokes, and of stories with a point, and always on the lookout for commissions, with a sharp eye to the margins of their customers.'**

TAKEN IN BY APPEARANCE

In the 'good old days' of a century ago, you could tell who was who in the City by their appearance.

> **'. . . the cashiers in private banking houses wore white hats and buff waistcoats; stockbrokers careered up Ludgate Hill in dog-carts – occasionally tandems – wearing sporty clothes; Jewish commission agents travelled in flashy broughams; and the men with millions were very shabby and wore very worn hats.'**

It seems that Bank of England clerks had the most luxuriant whiskers; and it was even rumoured that there was a 'whiskers club' within the precincts of the Bank.

Panmure Gordon, founder of that firm, drove to work in a four-in-hand, and his flamboyant appearance coincided with a flamboyant lifestyle.

He reputedly spent £2,000 a month on clothing, and had a pair of trousers for every day of the year.

The stiff collar was the uniform *de rigeur* in the City until relatively recently. Anyone caught wearing a soft collar risked being asked why he was wearing pyjamas. To Paul Getty, such stiff collars were simply an encumbrance – which he clearly avoided successfully: 'I've made many mistakes and miscalculations,' he remarked, 'on days when I'm wearing a tight collar.'

A picture of a banker of the so-called 'old school', written in the mid-19th century:

> 'He bore little resemblance to his modern successor: he was a man of serious manners, plain apparel, the steadiest conduct, and a rigid observer of formalities. As you looked in his face you could read . . . that the ruling maxim of his life, the one to which he turned all his thoughts, and by which he shaped all his actions, was, that he who would be trusted with the money of other men should look as if he deserved the trust and be an ostensible pattern to society of probity, exactness, frugality and decorum. He lived — if not the whole of the year, at least the greater part of the year — at his banking house; was punctual to the hours of business, and always to be found at his desk. The fashionable society at the West end of town, and the amusements of high life, he never dreamed of enjoying.'

And what is Wall Street?

'. . . a thoroughfare in name, but something more. To the banker and stock broker it is a financial center, collecting and distributing money, regulating the exchanges of a continent and striking balances of trade with London and Frankfort. To the outside observer and novice it is a kind of work-shop thronged by cunning artisans who work in precious metals, where vessels of gold and vessels of silver are wrought or made to shine with fresh luster, and where old china is fire-gilt as good as new. The moralist and philosopher look upon it as a gambling den — a cage of unclean birds, an abomination where men drive a horrible trade, fattening and battening on the substance of their friends and neighbours — or perhaps a kind of modern coliseum where gladiatorial combats are joined, and bulls, bears and other ferocious beasts gore and tear each other for the public amusement. The brokers regard it as a place of business where, in mercantile parlance, they may ply a legitimate trade, buying and selling for others on commission. To the speculators it is a caravanserai where they may load or unload their camels and drive them away betimes to some pleasant oasis. To the financial commanders it is an arsenal in which their arms and chariots are stored, the stronghold to be defended or beseiged, the field for strategy, battles and plunder . . .'

W. W. FOWLER, TWENTY YEARS OF INSIDE LIFE IN WALL STREET (1880)

Brahma bulls on Wall Street.

And Wall Street man?

As a species he (and now she) seems not to have changed much since this description of 100 years ago; mostly the language in which the emotions are couched would differ:

> 'His airy existence seems to be based in chasing the flying fractions up and down the market, or in making values which pass through his hands perspire gold drops. . .
>
> . . . amid the convolutions of his brain, a silent, invisible struggle is going on, which if put into bodily shape would startle the beholder. There the vulture passions are at work, led on by their generals, ambition and avarice. Pining envy, fear of an evil which always impends, rage over injuries inflicted by others or by his own weaknesses and incapacity, jealousy and hatred of successful rivals, all hold carnival in the space of an hour, and are kept active and sleepless by hope which quickens them with her enchanted wings.
>
> Above him hovers, day and night, a vast, dark, formless shape, threatening ruin and penury. This is the spectre of panic. One day he is lifted to dizzy heights, the next plunged into black depths. He is hurried through dark labyrinths, through paths where a single step is destruction. He climbs on the edge of a sword to a fool's paradise, where he tastes joys brief as a dream, and in an hour is abased to the earth where he drinks the full cup of humiliation and want.
>
> Meanwhile nature is holding out strange signals of alarm. His lips and cheeks blanch without any assignable cause. Blacksmiths' sparks flicker before his eyes. His blood regurgitates to his heart, which seems to swell to the size of a bullock's, and beats on his ribs like a trip hammer. Paralysis, apoplexy and aneurism are watching for their prey.'

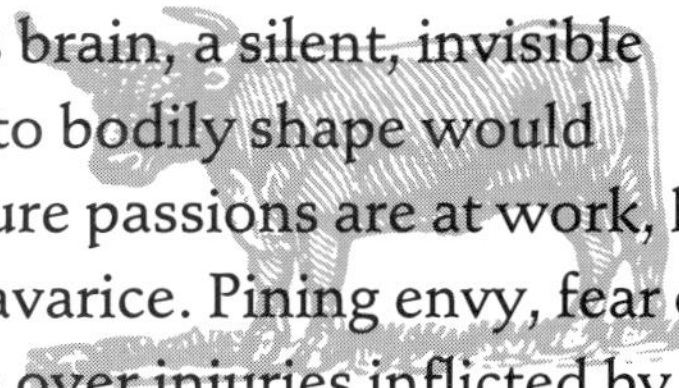

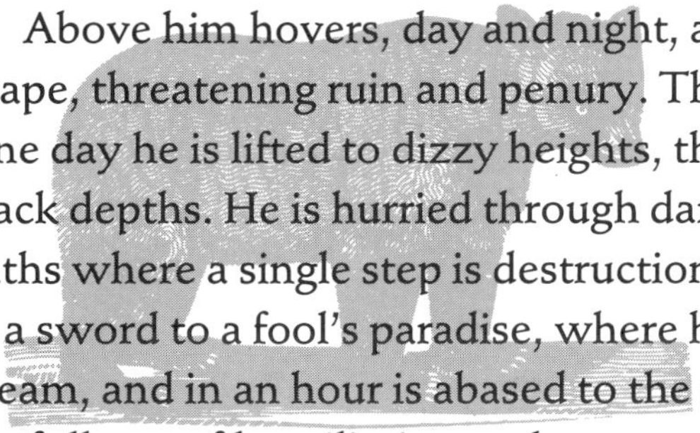

W. W. FOWLER, TWENTY YEARS OF INSIDE LIFE IN WALL STREET (1880)

'Count no Wall Street speculator rich till his estate has been settled.'

ANON

BEFORE TECHNOLOGY

With today's speed of technology, worldwide trading and instant information, we easily forget how time-consuming and complex business could be, just 100 years ago.

Pigeon expresses — the most efficient means of conveying information — expanded across Europe, and worked mostly from May to September. The birds used were generally the Antwerp breed, strong on the wing and fully feathered. One wonders what happened in the winter months.

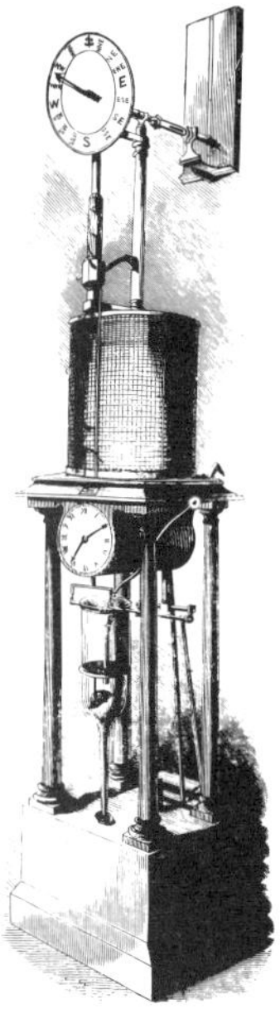

Lloyds (*c.* 1840)

'To assist the Lloyd's underwriters in their calculations, at the end of the Subscribers Room is an Anenometer, which registers the state of the wind day and night. Attached is a rain gauge.

On the roof of the Exchange is a sort of mast, at the top of which is a fan, like that of a windmill, the object of which is to keep a plate of metal with its face presented to the wind. Attached to this plate are springs which, joined to a rod, descend into the Underwriters room upon a large sheet of paper placed against the wall. To this end of the rod a lead pencil is attached, which slowly traverses the paper horizontally, by means of clock-work. When the wind blows very hard against the plate outside, the spring, being pressed, pushed down the rod and the pencil makes a long line down the paper vertically, which denotes a high wind. At the bottom of the sheet another pencil moves, guided by a vane on the outside, which so directs its course horizontally that the direction of the wind is shown. The sheet of paper is divided into squares, numbered with the hours of night and day, and the clock-work so moves the pencils that they take exactly an hour to traverse each square; hence the strength and direction of the wind at any hour of the 24 are easily seen.'

THE SELF ACTING STOCKBROKER'S BAROMETER.

The Clearing House (*c.* 1840)

'The Clearing House is fitted up with desks for each of the present twenty seven clearing bankers, whose names, taking the first of each name, are arranged in alphabetical order as follows, over each desk: Barclay, Barnard, Barnetts, Bosanquet, Brown, Curries, Denison, Dorrien, Fuller, Glyn, Hanbury, Hankey, Jones, Lubbock, Masterman, Prescot, Price, Robarts, Rogers, Smith, Spooner, Stevenson, Stone, Veres, Weston, Williams, Willis.

The rapidity with which the last charges are required to be entered, and the bustle which is created by their swift distribution through the room are difficult to be conceived. It is then, on the point of striking four, and on days of heavy business, that the beauty of the alphabetical arrangement of the clearers' desks is to be seen. All the distributors are moving in the same way round the room, with no further interference than may arise from the more active pressing upon or outstripping the slower of their fellow assistants. With equal celerity are their last credits entered by the clearers. A minute or two having passed, all the noise has ceased. The deputy clearers have left with the last charges on their houses; the clearers are silently occupied in casting up the amounts of the accounts in their books, balancing and entering the differences in their balance sheets until at length an announcement begins to be heard of the probable amounts to be received or paid, as a preparation for the final settlement. The four o'clock balances having been entered in the balance sheet, each clearer goes round to check and mark off his accounts with the rest, with 'I charge you' or 'I credit you' according as each balance is in his favour or against him.'

EVE'S CURIOSITY.

Young Wife: 'I wish you'd let me go with you to the City tomorrow, Fred!' Young Husband: 'Why, my love?' Young Wife: 'Because I should so like, just for once, to take a walk through the *Money-Market*!'

This 'traditional' view of women's capacity to understand finance pervaded the City until quite recently.

As late as 25 June 1971, 'The Thunderer' roared into print:

'IRRITATING AND OUT OF DATE'

'The Baltic Exchange, the shipbroking institution of the City of London is to be challenged on its rule excluding women from membership. This rule, as with the exclusion of women from the Stock Exchange, is an absurd anomaly. There is sometimes a tendency to regard these restrictions as a rather amusing anachronism, an endearing eccentricity, that cannot be defended logically but which does no real harm. Such a judgement is, however, quite mistaken. These are not private men's clubs going about their private activities. They are business institutions which exist to perform a public service, and they are institutions which have an effective monopoly in their respective fields.

There is therefore a public interest in this question in two quite separate respects. The first is that the exclusion of women from membership of these bodies imposes a barrier against the development of their personal career in those professions. It is a form of discrimination which has been abandoned in many other professions and which is increasingly regarded as intolerable unless it can be defended on specific practical grounds. It is hard to see what those grounds could be . . .

The second respect in which the public interest is affected by the exclusion of women from membership of the Baltic and Stock Exchange is that such a rule is a limitation upon the provision of professional services to the community. It is accordingly a restrictive practice . . . The Monopolies Commission on the professions concluded last October that 'the sex of the applicant should not be a condition of entry unless — as is likely to be the case very rarely indeed — there are particular circumstances . . .

If either the Stock Exchange or the Baltic is to qualify as one of these rare exceptions, it will have to provide a better justification than the reference to immemorial custom and prep school psychology . . .

This ridiculous situation has been allowed to continue for far too long already . . .'

Correspondence ensued during the next few days over whether the Stock Exchange and the Baltic were — or were not — private gentlemen's clubs or business institutions; and also whether the Stock Exchange in particular existed to perform a public service.

The Chairman of the Stock Exchange hastened to assure the readers that the Stock Exchange did perform a public service. Another reader wondered where the dining room and card room could be found if the Exchange was indeed a men's club.

TO SEE OURSELVES AS OTHERS SEE US

The play, 'Serious Money', a 'City Comedy', whose main location was '. . . LIFFE [which] appears as a bear garden of internationally linked phones and VDUs backed with a wall-length wine rack', played to packed audiences in London in 1987. A mostly City-based clientele enjoyed seeing their everyday dramas enacted on a somewhat smaller stage. At least as interesting as the play, however, were the comments it provoked from the reviewing critics. They used the opportunity to voice some widely-held views on the world of the City and its values:

> 'We are in a predatory world, where the clubby corruption of the old City is being replaced by the wolfish greed of the deregulated Eighties, and where the principle of survival is, as Comrade Trotsky so charmingly put it in another context, WHO WHOM.'
>
> Sunday Times

> '. . . a suavely complex financial horror cartoon, in which the pursuit of money lends life a savage, aphrodisiac energy, and where characters thrive or die according to their fitness for this gangster pace.'
>
> The Independent

The author herself, Caryl Churchill, commented:

> 'I still see the City as a lot of people making money at other people's expense, but I hadn't realised the extent of the attractiveness of it all.'

POTTED MONEY IN THE ATRIUMS OF WALL STREET

'History is repeating itself' claims John Kenneth Galbraith. 'The financial world is characterised by explosions of wealth and then, for those involved, a very sad day of reckoning. This has only lifted the process of financial aberration to new heights.'

The world's 'top earner' — of anyone anywhere, anytime, so thought the *New York Times* of 3 April 1989 — was Michael Milken, before his sudden demise. His 1987 income topped $550 million — which worked out at $1,047 per minute. Not even J. P. Morgan bettered that; that was his total wealth on his death in 1913. Was there something unbalanced in the financial system, pondered David Rockefeller. Maybe; in an era when a security analyst and a banker on Wall Street add to memorable money statements with such collectibles as . . . 'a million is kind of like peanuts now' . . . or 'the battleground for the top people on the street is between $2 million and $7 million.'

Even in modest London, salaries of £100,000 for 24-year-olds — 'but they can make a million for the firm in one phone call' — were rumoured in the mid-1980s. But this was before Black Monday, 19 October 1987. The salaries bubble had grown unabated — inevitably to burst. 'Earning your age' was no longer the theme tune — whether sung in pounds or dollars.

'Accumulate, accumulate! This is the golden rule of the capitalist economy.'

KARL MARX, 19th CENTURY

In memoriam for the unknown YUPPIE: The stock-market slide produced ready critics of City whiz-kids — but many forget these YUPPIES have brought wealth to us all.

SIMON JENKINS, SUNDAY TIMES, 25 OCTOBER 1987

'THIS HAS been a miracle month for the Great British Characteristic: smugness. Oh, the YUPPIES had it coming to them? Now let's watch them pawn their Porsches, drown in their CHAMPAGNE, rot in their second homes. Thank goodness the monstrous horde had only a year of glory before its demise. Thank goodness the market did not rally on Thursday. Thank goodness the whole disgusting business is over.

There were moments last week when I thought the media were going to choke on their own glee. By Thursday, writers sated on crashes, bears, busts and dippers were suffering acute metaphor fatigue. Shops sold out of books on 1929. Interviewers gurgled with pleasure as they questioned bemused analysts: hadn't we seen it coming, wasn't privatisation a con, what price now Mrs Thatcher's shareholder democracy, wasn't it all Ronald Reagan's fault, just how much poorer are the rich?

On Wednesday, the BBC's 9 o'clock News won the cliché-of-the-year award outright by actually leading its bulletin with 'Things can never be the same again'. After six months in purgatory, political Nemesis was back in her rightful place as top god in the Corporation's pantheon.

The British have always loathed markets and those who deal in them. Labour honours the 'honest' manufacturer and Tories the noble farmer and landowner. But financiers, competitors, market-makers have borne the stigmata of usury and trade. City money is fine, but only so long as it is genteel — and genteel means risk averse.

On this at least, Karl Marx was right. Capitalists have rarely been risk-seekers. They are risk-avoiders. They instinctively seek combination to fix price and exclude competition. Their natural habitat is the cartel. The old, pre-Big Bang City was the special creation of such men, a haven of restrictive practices and insider dealing, of private placings and baby syndicates. Wealth went to those who could ensure the highest profit for the low risk in direct proportion to loyalty to the club. Real financial innovation, options trading, futures discounting, the constant re-refining of the oil of commerce was best left to oils in the engine room. If they become too uppity they could be dismissed as spivs, speculators, asset strippers and YUPPIES. With a bit of luck, they could even be sent to jail.

But if Marx was right about capitalists, he was wrong about capitalism. Risk is its essence. Free-market capitalism is as much a trauma to most capitalists as full-blooded socialism is to most (probably to all) socialists. That is why the great risk-takers are seldom insiders. They are loners, innovators and adventurers. Their behaviour offends old money even more than no money because it threatens the cartel with competition. They are the shock of the new.

The YUPPIES projected into stardom over the past year by Big Bang and the boom in the securities market were in direct line of descent from the Tudor privateers and Victorian railway kings. Their ships may be swivel chairs and their iron horses video screens, but they work phenomenally hard and have ensured British financial services a pre-eminent role in a global growth industry. West German, Swiss and French stock markets have been left far behind. To achieve this, they have broken taboos and freed markets. Good luck to them if they also freed the market for their own labour. Just for once in the City, serious reward has been seen consorting with serious risk. The YUPPIES' critics are in direct line of descent too: from Shakespeare and his odious Merchant of Venice, from Dickens's tortured Dombey and Scrooge and, most savage of all, from Trollope's gruesome cast in The Way We Live Now. In this last, the ageing novelist hurled contempt on the YUPPIES who crowded London in 1873 to manipulate the bubble loans of the American world railway boom. (He forebore to mention that they also financed it.)

As his successors do today, Trollope tarred the risk-takers with the brush of fraud. They displayed a dishonesty 'magnificent in its

proportions, climbing into high places, so rampant and so splendid . . . with pictures on its walls, and gems in all its cupboards, with marble and ivory in all its corners.' At such a point wrote Trollope, dishonesty is so glamorised that 'it ceases to be abominable'. He protested that an alien Jewish financier should be greeted as an honoured guest at one of 'our' tables. It was the fault of that Disraeli.

True, the contemporaneity of the Guinness arrests and Black Monday has been a gift to the 'meanwhile elsewhere' school of journalism. It neatly equated speculative loss with accusations of theft. Super-greed may be present in financial markets as it is in most forms of economic activity. But while fraud may be a reflection of craven governments, it is no more a comment on risk capitalism than election-rigging is a comment on democracy.

That did not hamper last week's amateur Trollopes. Their glee has been directed not so much at the prospect of City poverty as at the threat this might pose to the envied YUPPIE LIFESTYLE. Who were these upstarts to mimic the leisure pursuits of their elders and betters? Some had risen from mere stockjobbers. Some were even women. Many had not been to university. What right had they to six-figure incomes, second homes, expensive cars and CHAMPAGNE on ice? These were perks normally confined to merchant bankers and Lloyd's underwriters. How typical that the YUPPIES should make their homes in vulgar Docklands and buy their cars from West Germany.

Contempt for the YUPPIES has come equally from conservatives of the right and left. The two most popular plays spawned by the bull market, Pravda and Serious Money, are riddled with it. Both are left-wing attacks not on the rich or well-born but on new money, on risk-takers who have dared to rise above their proper station. The pastiche villains are entrepreneurs of working-class or foreign origins, invariably portrayed as foul-mouthed and socially inept. Their virtuous antagonists have middle-class accents. Gone is the approached upward mobility of the 'kitchen-sink' school of drama. These are the most snobbish plays I have ever seen.

The young men and women of the City have been the advance guard of Britain's overdue capitalist revolution. They have assaulted reaction's strongest citadel and breached its walls. Small wonder their enemies view them with such disgust and take such pleasure in their current discomfort. May that pleasure be short-lived.'

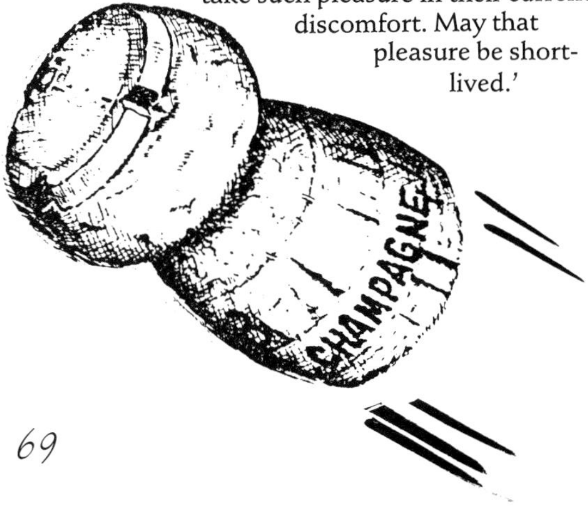

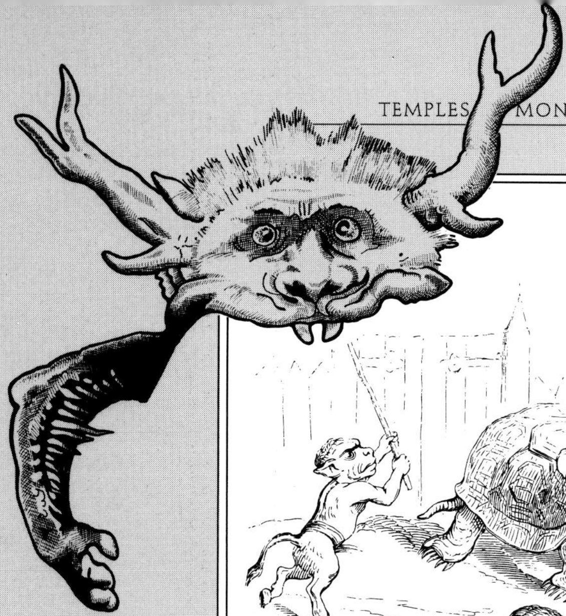

A FINANCIAL BESTIARY

The language of finance has grown ever more fanciful — particularly in the past ten years, with the growth of the futures and options markets.

Whereas bulls, bears and stags are terms which have been used in finance for over two hundred years, the new bestiary grows almost daily and includes real and imaginary sightings.

ALLIGATOR: a facetious Chicago phrase indicating an overly complex spread trade; one that eats the trader alive with transactions and commission costs at both ends.

AON: all-or-none order, ie, the order has to be completely filled or not at all.

BEAR: a person who believes that the market is in a downtrend.

BOTTOM FISHER: an investor who purchases stocks of companies that are at lows, usually bankrupt or near-bankrupt.

BULL: a person who believes the market is in an uptrend.

BUTTERFLY: a spread table in options, involving either buying/selling a low exercise price call, selling/buying two middle exercise price calls, and buying/ selling a high exercise price call.

CATS: an acronym for certificates of accrual on treasury securities.

CATERPILLAR: a spread trade of one butterfly against another.

COLTS: an acronym for 'continuously offered long-term securities'.

CONDOR: an option spread similar to a butterfly but without a common middle contract.

CUSIP: committee on uniform securities identification procedures.

FASTBACK: a debt security backed by auto loans; an acronym for 'first automotive short-term bonds and certificates'.

FOK: fill or kill order; trade order to be offered to market three times and if executed is cancelled.

GILT: UK government fixed interest security.

KILLER BEE: someone who aids a company in fending off takeover attempts by devising strategies to make the takeover target less attractive.

LYON: an acronym for 'liquid yield option notes' or zero coupon convertible bonds .

LIPPER GUAGE: the common term used for lipper mutual fund industry average.

OPOSSMS: an acronym for 'options to purchase or sell specific mortgage-backed securities'.

PTERADACTYL: same as a caterpillar.

SHARK: an entity in the process of trying to take over a targeted company.

STAG: term used to describe speculator who buys a new issue to sell shortly for profit.

TIGRS: an acronym for 'treasury investment growth receipts'.

TURKEY: an investment that not only did not perform as well as expected but went down in price as well.

The money spider (zool., a mite, the minute member of the Arachnida family) . . . *which brings financial luck, prosperity, and happiness* . . . or so the old saying goes.

CHAPTER 4

— BUBBLES, MANIAS AND PANICS —

'England is the country in which a spirit of adventure and speculation has done most to promote crises and depressions.'

THEODORE BURTON, 1902

In his famous study of crowd behaviour, in 1895, Gustave Le Bon commented that, upon becoming a member of a crowd, the individual 'descends several rungs in the order of civilisation'. A crowd feels invincible, is drawn by images, finds communication of feelings 'contagious', and is highly suggestible.

Individuals who form themselves into a crowd possess:

> '. . . a sort of collective mind which makes them feel, think and act in a manner quite different from that in which each individual one of them would feel, think and act were he in a state of isolation.'

This 'fever' which overtakes people has been prompted by various stimuli over the centuries: gold, tulips, fictitious companies and simple rumour.

> 'Much has been written about panics, manias and much more than with the most outstretched intellect we are able to follow or conceive; but one thing is certain, that at particular times a great deal of stupid people have a great deal of stupid money . . . At intervals, from causes which are not to the present purpose, the money of these people — the blind capital, as we call it, of the country — is particularly large and craving; it seeks for someone to devour it, and there is a plethora; it finds someone, and there is "speculation"; it is devoured, and there is "panic".'

WALTER BAGEHOT, ESSAY ON EDWARD GIBBON (19th CENTURY)

The Wheel of Fortune, Hogarth.

JOHN MAYNARD KEYNES, 20th CENTURY

'[the professional investor and speculator] are largely concerned not with making superior long term forecasts of the probable yield of an investment over its whole life, but with foreseeing changes in the conventional basis of valuation a short time ahead of the general public . . . it is, so to speak, a game of Snap, of Old Maid, of Musical Chairs — a pastime in which he is victor who says Snap neither too soon nor too late, who passes the Old Maid to his neighbour before the game is over, who secures a chair for himself when the music stops. These games can be played with zest and enjoyment, though all the players know that it is the Old Maid which is circulating, or that when the music stops some of the players will find themselves unseated.'

TULIPMANIA: 1634-37

Little to do with gardening or love of flowers, and all to do with speculation. Tulips, probably originating in Turkey (their name may be a derivation of 'dulban', a turban), were brought to Vienna by the Austrian ambassador to the Sultan's court in Constantinople. The curious flower created a great stir and found its way to Germany and Belgium, and to England in the early 1580s. It became popular in court and fashionable circles. In Paris, ladies even replaced the jewels on their dresses with tulip flowers.

Their popularity and relative scarcity made them objects of some speculation. The aim was to obtain unusual colours, or better still striped flowers with curled and fringed petals. By the 1620s rare specimens in the Netherlands were reaching thousands of florins. The craze spread, and soon even 'simpler' homes were beginning to turn over much of their cultivable land to the growing of tulip bulbs.

Soon, bulbs were being sold and traded in inns and clubs frequented by tulip traders. By 1634 deals were being conducted all year round, for delivery the following Spring: put and call options were invented in the process, the speculator having no intention of actually acquiring the bulb, but merely passing on the contract for its ownership as soon as possible, with as great a profit as possible. Special tulip notaries were created, but no member firm existed to 'confirm' these contracts, and there was no guarantee that the final purchaser would even receive what he had paid for.

As one observer put it: 'Before the tulip season was over, more roots were sold and purchased, bespoke and promised to be delivered than in all probability were to be found in all the gardens of Holland.'

As the frenzy mounted, and prices rose, other economic activity was neglected. Estates were mortgaged; in one supreme folly, a 'Viceroy' bulb sold for four oxen, eight pigs, twelve sheep, four loads of rye and two of wheat, two hogsheads of wine and four barrels of beer, two barrels of butter and half a ton of cheese, together with a bed, some clothes and a silver beaker — a total value of 2,500 florins. A 'Semper Augustus' — with vertical red and white stripes over a bluish inner hue — sold for about twice that value in cash plus a carriage and horses. And in France a single rare bulb was given as full payment for a successful brewery.

In The Hague, a cobbler produced a black tulip. He was visited by a group of tulip growers from Haarlem, who bought it from him for 1,500 florins, and promptly destroyed it. They too possessed one such bulb and were determined to protect its uniqueness. They later admitted they would have paid up to 10,000 florins if necessary for the privilege.

> 'There is nothing so disastrous as a rational investment policy in an irrational world.'
>
> *JOHN MAYNARD KEYNES*

By 1637, many small-time growers were flooding the market, prices began to fall, and by the summer buyers were reneging on their contracts. To try and stem the financial blows, representatives of many cities met and agreed that buyers should be permitted to cancel contracts for sales after November, but this led to massive litigation and court cases. By April the courts had become involved. It was decided that sellers who could not force their buyers to buy should accept any price, and sue the original buyer. In the process a great many families were ruined.

ONE MAN'S GOLD RUSH

On hearing that the Dutch fleet was sailing up the Thames in June 1667 — having already captured the Royall Charles, the ship in which Charles II had returned to England seven years previously — Samuel Pepys chose to bury his gold. Fearing that 'the whole kingdom is undone', he hastened to pack his father and wife off to the country, with all the family gold in their night bag:

> 'Pray God give them good passage and good care to hide it when they come home, but my heart is full of fear. They gone, I continued in frights and fears of what to do with the rest.
>
> W. Hewer [a life-long] friend hath been at the banquiers and hath got 500L out of Backewell's hands of his own money; but they are so called upon that they will be all broke, hundreds coming to them for money — and their answer is 'It is payable at twenty days; when the days are out, we will pay you' . . . I cannot have my 200 pieces of gold again for silver, all being bought up last night that were to be had — and sold for 24 and 25s-a-piece. So I must keep the silver by me . . .
>
> . . . I did about noon resolve to send Mr. Gibson [his clerk] away after my wife with another 1000 pieces . . . and did send my two silver flagons to Kate Joyce's . . . I have also made a girdle by which with some trouble I do carry about me 300L in gold about my body . . .'

A few days later he was 'mad' at his father's method of burying the gold:

> 'My father and she [his wife] did it on Sunday when they were gone to church, in open daylight in the midst of the garden, where for aught they knew many eyes might see them . . .'

The Dutch danger passed, in October he was able to retrieve his precious gold:

> '. . . my father and I with a dark lantern, it being now night, into the guarden with my wife and there went about our great work to dig up my gold. But Lord what a tosse I was for some time in, that they could not justly tell where it was, that I begun heartily to sweat and be angry that they should not agree better upon the place, and at last to fear that it was gone; but by and

by, poking with a spit, we found it, and then begun with a spudd to lift up the ground; but good God, to see how sillily they did it, not half a foot under ground and in the sight of the world from a hundred places if anybody by accident were near-hand, and within sight of a neighbour's window and their hearing also, being close by . . .

. . . but I was out of my wits almost, and the more from that upon my lifting up the earth with the spud, I did discern that I scattered the pieces of gold round about the ground among the grass and loose earth . . . I perceive that the earth was got among the gold and wet, so that the bags were all rotten, all the notes, that I could not tell what in the world to say to it, not knowing how to judge what was wanting, and what had been lost by Gibson . . . and at last was forced to take up the head pieces, dirt and all, and as many of the scattered pieces as I could with the dirt discern by candlelight, and carry them up into my brother's chamber and there lock them up till I had eat a littel supper: and then all people going to bed, W. Hewer and I did all alone, with several pales of water and basins, at last wash the dirt off of the pieces and parted the pieces and the dirt, and then begun to tell, and by a note which I had of the value of the whole (in my pocket) do find that there was short above 100 pieces which did make me mad . . . W. Hewer out again about midnight and there by candlelight did make shift to gather 45 pieces more — and so in and to cleanse them and by this time it was 2 in the morning; and so to bed.'

The operation was resumed the next morning; and he took the 10 o'clock coach back to London: 'my gold I put into a basket and set under one of the seats'.

'To have money is a fear;
to not have it is a grief.'

G. HERBERT, 1640

SOUTH SEA COMPANY (OR 'BUBBLE')

'a mighty fabric founded on fraud, illusion, credulity and infatuation.'

Founded in 1711 by the Earl of Oxford, the company was initially spoken of as 'the Earl of Oxford's masterpiece', and took over part of the national debt amounting to around £10 million. The Government was to pay 6 per cent interest annually, from duties levied on certain luxurious items such as tobacco, whalefins, wrought silks and wines.

The inevitable origins of the 'Bubble' lay in the monopoly that the company was granted on trade with the South Seas — disregarding the fact that Spain had no intention of allowing free trade with what were, at that period, her possessions. The prime attractions to investors, however, were the gold and silver — believed to be inexhaustible — from the mines of Mexico and Peru.

In 1720, riding on its successes, the company offered to take over the entire national debt of £30 million. The price of the stock rose from £130 to £350, and access to Exchange Alley was blocked by crowds wanting to buy South Sea Company stock. Tables appeared in the Alley to deal with the onslaught, and between 1 May and 3 June 1720 the price of stock rose from £500 to £890, proceeding on to £1,000, before falling to £640 in September, hurtling downwards to £135, and ruining hundreds in its wake, but rewarding those who got out in time.

By the end of April 1720, the Dutch banker Crellius exclaimed that Exchange Alley resembled 'nothing so much as if all the lunatics had escaped out of the madhouse at once'. In June and July there were twelve-hour relays between London and Amsterdam, and on 16 July some eighty Jewish Presbyterians and Anabaptists, all speculators on Exchange Alley, were off to Holland and Hamburg to mend their fortunes by speculating on the continental insurance stocks.

The poet Alexander Pope lost half his investment; the playwright John Gay — according to Dr Johnson — lost all his shares; Thomas Guy sold his shares in time, made £234,000, and spent a proportion of his gains on building the hospital which now bears his name; and Robert Walpole, later prime minister, sold out in time, at the top of the market, and rebuilt his stately home. The Prince of Wales and the Duke of Argyll were equally lucky, but Sir David Hamilton, the royal physician, lost £80,000. The Chancellor of the Exchequer, John Aislabie, made an illegal profit of £794,000 — and following the investigation into the affairs of the Company, was conveyed to the Tower for his troubles .

Sir Isaac Newton, the famous physicist and the Master of the Royal Mint claimed: 'I can calculate the motions of the bodies, but not the maddness of people'. On 20 April he accordingly sold his shares in the Company at a solid 100 per cent profit. Unhappily for him, a further impulse seized him, he re-entered the market at the top for a larger amount, and ended up losing £20,000.

Imitators of such fabulous speculative schemes multiplied: Briscoe's transmutations of animals, Mother Wyebourne's Machine Conundrums, Pollington's plan to 'melt' sawdust to deal-boards, schemes to cure lunatics and broken-winded horses, an office for maintaining bastard children, a hair-trading enterprise, a coral fishery, a company for radish oil, and many more, including an undertaking 'of great promise', but what it was would not be revealed until 'due time', in the meantime share owners to pay two guineas a share. The perpetrator made off with £2,000, keeping his secret and failing to meet investors.

'Subscribers here by thousands float,
And jostle one another down,
Each paddling in his leaky boat,
And here they fish for gold, and drown.

Now buried in the depths below,
Now mounted up to heaven again,
They reel and stagger to and fro
At their wit's end, like drunken men.

Meantime, secure on Garraway cliffs,
A savage race, by shipwrecks fed,
Lie waiting for the founder'd skiffs
And strip the bodies of the dead.'

JONATHAN SWIFT, BALLAD ON THE SOUTH SEA SCHEME (1721)

RUE QUINCAMPOIX

A narrow street in Paris where investors in John Law's Mississippi Scheme gathered round his house to buy shares.

The scheme itself — to establish a company with exclusive trading rights on the Mississippi river and in Louisiana — was sound, and based on Law's already well-established reputation as a reliable financier. However, the speculation it engendered overtook it and sound sense. The main initial problem was the production of paper bank notes without adequate backing.

However, investors crowded the street, anxious to invest in so profitable a scheme; and the local inhabitants made the most of it. Houses previously rented at 800 livres a year were now going for between 6,000 and 16,000 livres a month; the local cobbler built a stall, provided pen and paper, and managed to earn 200 livres a day from brokers and their clients; by providing chairs he gained more from ladies interested in watching the proceedings in comfort.

Law was forced to move to Place Vendôme, with the crowds still in attendance. Booths and tents were erected in the Place, and gamblers with roulette tables gained their share of the business to be made.

The company lasted some two years before people began to feel pangs of alarm at possessing ever more paper money, not immediately exchangeable into precious metal.

◆

Martin Luther, the 16th-century Protestant church reformer, was presented with four mining shares. He exclaimed:

> **'I want no shares! This is speculative money, and I will not make this kind of money multiply.'**

◆

DESCRIPTION OF THE AMSTERDAM STOCK EXCHANGE, 1688

'A typical speculator ". . . chews his nails, pulls his fingers, closes his eyes, takes four paces, and four times talks to himself, raises his hand to his cheek as if he has a toothache and all this accompanied by a mysterious coughing".'

THE BUBBLERS MEDLEY, or a SKETCH of the TIMES
Being EUROPES MEMORIAL for the YEAR 1720.
Si Populus vult Decipi Decipiatur
Mint Coffe House
The Dutch Bubblers
The Dutch, who once were thought to be,
A crafty Generation,
Are grown as foolish now we see,
As any Neighb'ring Nation;
They coppy England, England, France,
In vile destructive Bubbles,
And e'ery idle fraud advance,
That can augment their troubles.
Three Nations sure were never curs'd,
Before with such a Madness,
That raises joyfull hopes at first,
But terminates in Sadness.
QUINQUEMPOIX STREET.
Behold the famous Pile where Law of late,
Bubbl'd the Publick to enrich the State,
But Traytor like when he ye Work had done,
(Was glad to Fly the Peoples rage to shun;
Some say for safety he is fled to Rome,
Yet let us not reflect but look at home.
Twixt France & us this difference is found;
Their Bubblers run but ours must stand the ground
Grieve not my friends tis but a merry farce
To hear ye Kettle call ye Pot black Arse.
Stock Jobbing Cards or the Humours of Change Alley
The London Ga
By Authority.
to Tuesday August 16. 1720.
Whitehall, Aug. 10 1720
York Buildings Company,
Lustring Company
English Copper
Welsh Copper and Lead
Printed by S. Buckley
Bubble Poem
There is a Gulf where Thousands fell,
Here all the bold Adventrers came;
A Narrow Sound, tho' Deep as Hell,
'Change Alley is the dreadfull Name.
Nine times a Day it Ebbs and Flows,
Yet he that on the Surface lies,
Without a Pilot seldom knows
The time it Fall, or when twill Rise.
Subscribers here by Thousands float,
And justle one another down,
Each padling in his leaky Boat,
And here they fish for Gold and drown.
Now burry'd in the Depth below,
Then mounted up to Heav'n again;
They Reel and Stagger to and fro,
At their Wits end, like Drunken Men.
Mean time secure on Garr'way's Cliffs,
A Savage Race by Shipwrecks fed,
Lye waiting for the founder'd Skiffs,
And strip the Bodies of the Dead.
As Fishes on each other Prey,
The Great Ones Swallowing up the Small,
So fares it in the Southern Sea;
But Whale Directors Eat up all.
While some build Castles in the Air,
Directors build 'em in the Seas;
Subscribers plainly see 'em there,
For Fools will see as Wise Men please.
Thus by Directors we are told,
Pray Gentlemen believe your Eyes;
Our Ocean's cover'd o'er with Gold,
Look round about how thick it lies.
Oh! would these Patriots be so kind,
Here in the Deep to wash their Hands;
Then like Pactolus, we should find,
The Sea indeed had Golden Sands.
The Nation too too late will find,
Computing all their Cost and Trouble,
Directors Promises but Wind,
South Sea at best a mighty Bubble.
22
Printed for CARINGTON BOWLES, N°.69 in St. Pauls Church Yard, London.

CALIFORNIAN GOLD

The 'forty-niners' who headed for California found the going rough: the spotting of gold dust and pellets 'about half the size of a pea' by the first prospectors was enough for the spawning of the apocryphal tale of the elder Mormon, Sam Brannan, rushing through the streets of San Francisco holding a bottle full of nuggets shouting 'Gold! Gold! Gold! on the American river' . . . and the rush was on. Waggons, mules, oxen and shuffling feet toiled and trudged into the Sierras of California. Using shovels, picks and pans they sifted sand and water to catch the minutest pieces of gold dust. One group found a nugget worth $278; that paled into insignificance when one man took out $1,500-worth in an hour; and three Frenchmen found $5,000-worth under a tree-stump.

On hearing of the bonanza, Europeans took to the oceans.

THE CALIFORNIAN MOVEMENT.

They anticipated a successful return journey . . . but

> 'intelligence from California is unfortunately not of a nature to tempt the reflective emigrant, since, upon a fair calculation, it is shown that though a working man may earn one hundred dollars per day, he must spend ninety-nine in purchasing the necessaries of life — leaving a balance of one for luxuries, or for coming home again'.

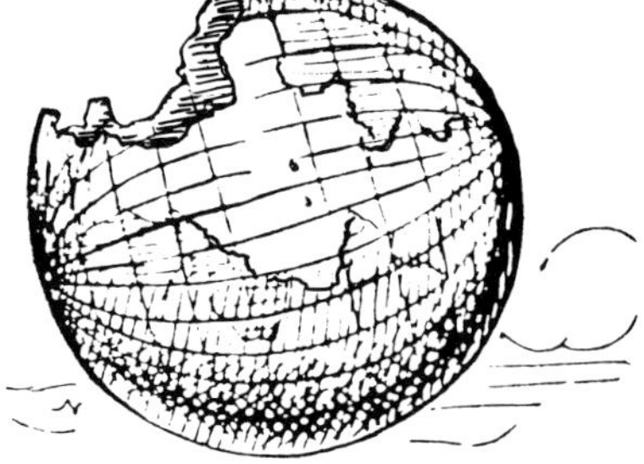

THE EARTH, AT THE END OF THE DIGGINGS.

Four years later, everyone was heading for Australia, where gold diggings were rewarding the patient — and the lucky — with amazing wealth.

THE ROAD TO RUIN.

RAILWAY MANIA

George Stephenson's invention of the 1820s, the steam engine, caught the public's fancy. An ideal way of travelling, its potential as a new form of business — railway companies to link the entire country — soon became the object of much speculation.

In one week in 1845, eighty-nine new schemes were announced, with a capital of over £84 million; within a month, there were 350 more, with a capital of £330 million.

Revenues from advertising these railway ventures netted considerable sums for the newspapers of the day. Leading journals, it has been estimated, received £12,000-£14,000 a week from this source, with double page advertisements and special insertions describing the scope and advantages of each scheme.

All travelled smoothly, until the panic of October, a panic:

> '. . . fatal to the middle class. It reached every hearth, it saddened every heart in the metropolis. Entire families were ruined. Scarcely an important town in England but what beheld some wretched suicide . . . daughters delicately nurtured went out to seek their bread; sons recalled from academies; . . . debtors' jails peopled with promoters . . .'

A VIEW FROM THE STREET: THE CRASH OF 1929

'There has been a little distress selling on the stock exchange due to a technical condition of the market.'

THOMAS LAMONT, SENIOR PARTNER OF BANKER J. P. MORGAN (THURSDAY, 24 OCTOBER 1929)

During the previous day, the last hour of trading had seen 2.6 million shares change hands at plummeting prices. The panic continued over the next few days, not helped by bad communications between New York and the rest of the country — a combination of too few wires to cope with the volume of business, with the ensuing disparity between ticker-tape prices and those actually on the floor, and appalling weather conditions across the mid-West.

In the city itself, crowds rushed to the visitors' gallery at the Exchange, where, in the words of one commentator '. . . they witnessed bedlam. Some onlookers wept and others screamed — while brokers themselves were in tears and hoarse with shouting'.

Worse was to come. On 'Black Tuesday', 29 October, over 3 million shares were sold in the first half hour of trading. By the end of the day that figure was 16 million.

'If you see a banker jump out of a window, follow him; there's bound to be a profit in it.'

VOLTAIRE, 18th CENTURY

The 1929 Wall Street Crash was full of rumours of this advice being followed by one and all, but any evidence of it actually happening is very tenuous.

Rumours, however, claimed that eleven bankers had already taken this headlong plunge into the unknown, as early as 24 October. There was even a claim that two speculators had jumped hand in hand from the Ritz '. . . because they had a joint account'. For some time thereafter, hotel receptionists supposedly asked people . . . 'do you want a room for sleeping in, or jumping from?'

CROWDS SEE MARKET HISTORY MADE

CROWDS AT TICKERS SEE FORTUNES WANE

Other Investors Sit Silently in Brokerages and Watch Movies of Disappearing Gains.

CAMARADERIE IN TRAGEDY

Throng at Exchange, Eager to Be Near as Market History is Made, but Scene on Floor is Orderly.

Groups of men, with here and there a woman, stood about inverted glass bowls all over the city yesterday watching spools of ticker tape unwind and as the tenuous paper with its cryptic numerals grew longer at their feet their fortunes shrunk. Others sat stolidly on tilted chairs in the customers' rooms of brokerage houses and watched a motion picture of waning wealth as the day's quotations moved silently across a screen.

It was among such groups as these, feeling the pulse of a feverish financial world whose heart is the Stock Exchange, that drama and perhaps tragedy were to be found. On the floor of the Exchange itself there was little to indicate that the butcher, the baker and the candlestick maker, all were dumping holdings upon a market whose buying appetite was sated.

But the crowds about the ticker tapes, like friends about the bedside of a stricken friend, reflected in their faces the story the tape was telling. There were no smiles. There were no tears either. Just the camaraderie of fellow-sufferers. Everybody wanted to tell his neighbor how much he had lost. Nobody wanted to listen. It was too repetitious a tale.

Crowds Outside Exchange

Crowds gathered about the chaste white building that is the Stock Exchange, drawn by the fascination of being close while financial history was being made, to catch the fever of excitement that emanated from it. Many who stopped at Broad and Wall Streets knew not why they had come or what they had hoped to see. Actually they saw little enough—bankers whom they did not know by sight hurrying in and out of the office of J. P. Morgan & Co. across the way, other sightseers, a special detail of policemen and a few political speakers who addressed the noonday crowds near the Sub-Treasury Building.

Inside the Exchange, from which all visitors have been barred since Thursday's break in prices, the scene was only a little more dramatic. Even in the closing rally, when excitement reached the high pitch for the day, the scene was not so different from that beneath the grandstand at race meets when bettors hurry to lay their wagers with bookmakers before the bugle sounds. In calmer moments the floor resembled Grand Central Terminal at commuting time with the information desk multiplied many times.

Richard Whitney, acting president of the Exchange, hat tilted on his head at a jaunty angle, sauntered nonchalantly across the floor half an hour before the closing and left the room with a debonair smile at Post 2, where traders in United States Steel, one of the country's basic industries, were waiting to dispose of shares at 175. It closed Monday at 186 and dropped yesterday at one time to 170.

Growing Excitement at Close.

The hands of the clock on the west wall moved steadily around towards 3 o'clock, the hour of closing. Time was growing short. Little groups of brokers went into huddles around the posts where the more active issues, General Electric, Steel, Anaconda, were being bought and sold. The hoarse undertone that wailed up from the floor increased in volume. Occasionally it was pierced by a whistle, a shriek. A few hands were upraised as bidding for stocks began. It looked like what it was—a rally.

Amid this growing turmoil the clock's hands crept steadily around toward the right angle of 3 o'clock—the hour when the broker's work is done and the hour when the troubles of his clerical force in the office begin. William Crawford, a dark-haired youth who is superintendent of the mechanical department which reports the record of sales and prices, sauntered out upon the marble rostrum, sat down and took a watch from his pocket.

The tumult of shouting increased. The whole tempo of the scene speeded up. The small man in gray continued his calisthenic bidding. The first stroke of the closing gong came at fifteen seconds of 3. The last choked off a shouted offer and reduced the bedlam to a murmur. Slowly, singly the brokers surrendered the floor to the porters to sweep up the torn papers, which littered it so thickly as to form a carpet.

M. C. Bouvier and William B. Wodsworth, who welcomed him as a member in 1869, left the floor showing fewer signs of strain than brokers half their age, although they had been more active in the trading than in many years.

As soon as word of the sensational drop in prices which marked the opening of the Exchange, reached Police Headquarters, Commissioner Whalen, anticipating crowds of sightseers in the financial district, ordered thirty extra patrolmen and four mounted policemen to proceed to the neighborhood of Broad and Wall Streets.

The turnover of more than 16,000,000 shares in a day's trading swamped the machinery of the financial world. The clerical forces of brokers' offices were held with their noses at their ledgers until long after midnight. The sidewalks teemed with scurrying runners, clutching comparison slips in their hands. Hundreds of taxicabs lined the curbs in Wall Street, Broad Street and Exchange Place.

Restaurants in the financial district, which usually close early in the evening remained open until midnight and virtually all their tables were filled. The office buildings themselves were as brightly illuminated as at 5 P.M. on an ordinary day.

THE NEW YORK TIMES, WEDNESDAY 30 OCTOBER, 1929

CHAPTER 5

— MONEY AS A POSSESSION —

'Money is human happiness in the abstract. He, then, who is no longer capable of enjoying human happiness in the concrete devotes himself utterly to money.'

A. SCHOPENHAUER, 19th CENTURY

Some 1600 years before Schopenhauer wrote those lines, Aristotle was refining his thoughts on the distinction between two forms of money-making: one 'natural' because it was directed to the primary purpose of obtaining objects for daily living; the other 'unnatural' because it was directed at accumulation of wealth — 'a quantity of coins' — and as such knew no limits.

The desire to accumulate money is like a many-tentacled fungus: it spreads into every crack and crevice.

As Seneca pointed out some twenty centuries ago:

> 'Our parents have trained us to admire gold and silver, and the love of it has grown up with us to such a degree that when we need to show our gratitude to Heaven, we make presents of these metals.
>
> It is this that makes poverty look like a curse and a reproach, and the poets have perpetuated this: the chariot of the Sun must be of gold; the best of times must be the golden age; and thus they turn the greatest misery of mankind into the greatest blessing.'

SENECA, MORALS (1st CENTURY AD)

For the Roman Emperor, Caligula, money had a rather idiosyncratic attraction. Highly extravagant and hence constantly impoverished, his daughter's birth gave him yet another excuse to complain of poverty:

> ' In addition to the burden of sovreignty,' he said, 'I must now shoulder that of fatherhood', and promptly took up a collection for her education and dowry. He also announced that New Year gifts would be welcomed on 1 January; and then sat in the Palace porch, grabbing the handfuls and lapfuls of coins which a mixed crowd of all classes pressed on him. At last he developed a passion for the feel of money, and spilling heaps of gold pieces on an open space, would walk over them barefoot, or else lie down and wallow.'

SUETONIUS, TWELVE CAESARS (1st CENTURY AD), ed. ROBERT GRAVES

The American industrialist and millionaire, Andrew Carnegie, writing in his diary in December 1868, foresaw what dangers lurked for him:

> 'Man must have an idol — the amassing of wealth is one of the worst species of idolatry — no idol more debasing than the worship of money. Whatever I engage in I must push inordinately; therefore should I be careful to choose that life which will be the most elevating in its character. To continue much longer overwhelmed by business cares and with most of my thoughts wholly upon the way to make more money in the shortest time must degrade me beyond hope of permanent recovery.'

'If you make money your god, it will plague you like the Devil.'

H. FIELDING, 18th CENTURY

We day-dream of possessing endless riches and wealth, imagining they will resolve our problems, fulfil all our wishes, and give us peace of mind. We have invented folk-tales about geese laying golden eggs, and magic stones turning everything to gold . . . in our endless pursuit for the ideal. If we had one wish, what would it be?

In antiquity, King Midas was confronted with the same question. In return for a good deed — wining and feasting Silenus, the rotund companion of the god Bacchus — the latter offered him a gift: 'anything you desire shall be granted to you'. Without much thought, Midas opted for gold: 'let everything I touch turn to gold'.

Bacchus sadly agreed to this wish — for he knew it would bring nothing but sadness. But Midas was overjoyed and immediately tried out his new-found power. He broke off a twig from a small oak tree; it immediately turned to gold. Hardly daring to believe his luck, he picked up a pebble, which also turned a lustrous gold. Next, a clod of earth changed into a nugget, and ears of corn became sheaths of the wondrous metal. Even running water in which he washed his hands transformed into gleaming sheets of gold. He was happy beyond the dreams of avarice.

But happiness has an elusive quality. His first meal of fine meats and wine turned to inedible slices of hard gold. His joy began to wane. After many days, and parched with thirst and weakened with hunger, he turned again to Bacchus: 'take pity on me, I beg. Your gift is not what I had expected.'

The god again acquiesced, and told Midas to bathe in the river Pactolus that flowed past the city of Sardis — which to this day bears the specks of gold that were washed from Midas' body.

'I'm tired of love, I'm tired of Rhyme
But money gives me pleasure all the time.'

HILAIRE BELLOC, FATIGUED

J. Gy. inv & f. Pubd. March 9th 1797. by H. Humphrey New Bond Street

MIDAS, Transmuting all, into ~~GOLD~~ PAPER.

History of Midas, — The great Midas having dedicated himself to Bacchus, obtained from that Deity, the Power of changing all he Touched. Apollo fixed Asses Ears upon his head, for his Ignorance — & although he tried, to hide his disgrace with a Regal Cap, yet the very Sedges which grew from the Mud of the Pactolus, whisperd out his Infamy, whenever they were agitated by the Wind from the opposite Shore. — Vide Ovid's Metamorphoses

A 19th-century French cartoon depicts the Devil, the patron of finance, dispensing largesse.

Churchmen have for centuries condemned money-making as the work of Satan. St Francis renounced it, and urged his followers to do likewise.

John Wesley, in an 18th-century sermon, 'The Use of Money', took a more pragmatic approach:

> 'Gain all you can without hurting either yourself or your neighbour . . . save all you can by cutting off every expense which serves only to indulge foolish desire . . . waste nothing, living or dying, on sin or folly, whether for yourself or your children; and then give all you can or in other words, give all you have to God.'

MONEY . . . THE NEW MORALITY

Fourteenth-century Italy — home to some of the earliest and most successful banks which developed European networks — also created some of the more cynical views of this money-making and grabbing urge . . . which has echoes in today's world of high finance.

> 'The world is so base nowadays that wisdom and noble stock are worth nothing unless they are mixed with money, which condiments and seasons every good dish . . . so let him who has money know how to hold onto it, if he wants to avoid being told one day: 'I can't bear the sight of you'.'

THE ITALIAN POET TEBALDI, EARLY 14th CENTURY

◆

'Money makes the man.
Money makes the stupid pass for bright,
Money buys the treasury of sins,
Money shows;
Money buys the pleasure-giving women,
Money keeps the soul in bliss,
Money puts the plebe in high estate,
Money brings your en'mies down;
And every man seems down without it,
The world and fortune being ruled by it . . .'

NICCOLO ROSSI, 14th-CENTURY NOBLEMAN FROM TREVISO

◆

'While money can't buy you everything,
it certainly puts you in a good bargaining position.'

A. H. BERZEN, WALL STREET JOURNAL (1989)

John Maynard Keynes, in writing his essay 'The economic possibilities for our grandchildren' (1931), pondered the millenium as a golden age, when:

> **'. . . the love of money as a possession — as distinguished from love of money as a means to the enjoyments and realities of life — will be recognised for what it is: a somewhat disgusting morbidity, one of those semi-criminal, semi-pathological propensities which one hands over with a shudder to the specialists in mental disease.'**

Miserliness is just one expression of this morbidity. Folklore — with its moral teachings — has given us several examples: the miser who tries to eat his gold and chokes to death . . . or the treasure chest which falls on the miser and kills him.

Charles Dickens' Scrooge — "a squeezing, wrenching, grasping, scraping, clutching, covetous old sinner" — is probably the best-known 'literary' miser.

Engrossed in his one master-passion — gain — and weighing everything against it, he is visited by the restless ghost of his erstwhile partner, Marley. With the benefit of hindsight, he warns Scrooge of the fate that awaits such a friendless, avaricious spirit.

"My spirit never walked beyond our counting-house . . . in my life my spirit never roved beyond the narrow limits of our money-changing hole; and weary journeys lie before me."

THE RICH MISER

'Once upon a time there was a man who was very rich but got no pleasure out of it.

One night he went to bed but could not fall asleep for thinking that though he was rich the tsar was richer still.

"Why does the tsar, who has more than enough silver and gold, tax people and take away their money?" he asked himself. "Now, if I were a little richer than I am, not only would I be happy myself but I would help the poor and make them happy too."

All of a sudden he heard a voice whisper in his ear:

"There is a bag beside you with only one silver coin in it. Take out the coin, and another will appear in its place. In this way you will be able to get as many silver coins as you like. When you feel that you have enough, throw the bag into the river, and you will then be able to use them. If you leave the bag with you, the coins will turn to stones."

The man was overjoyed. He looked, and lo! — there was a bag beside him. Reaching into it hurriedly, he brought out a silver coin. He put it on his bed, reached into the bag for the second time and brought out another coin. And so it continued.

"I'm really lucky for once!" the rich man cried, feeling very happy indeed.

He spent the whole night taking the coins out of the bag and by morning had piles and piles of them. He then decided that he would throw the bag into the river as soon as the sun was out and would then spend part of the money on himself and give the rest to the poor. But he changed his mind when the sun appeared and told himself that he had better take another day to collect more coins. "And I won't take time off to eat," he said. "I can do without food for a day."

But the more coins he took out of the bag the more he wanted and no sooner had he taken out one than he found himself reaching for another. He

was very hungry, but dared not stop or leave the magic bag for even a minute.

A week went by and then a month, and a year, and he was still at it, and he found comfort in the thought that anyone in his place would have rejoiced to be able to get so much money so easily. In his greed he forgot both himself and the poor he had once thought to help. There were times when he would set out with the bag for the river only to turn back again at the thought that once it was in the water he would get no more coins out of it.

Many years passed, and the rich man grew old and sick, but he went on taking the coins out of the bag and never stopped. And at last there came a day when he was found beside a mountain of silver coins, dead, his fingers still clutching the bag.'

UKRAINIAN FOLK-TALE

'I love liberty; I hate embarrassment, worry and subjection. So long as the money lasts in my purse, it assures me of independence and relieves me of the need of plotting to obtain more, a need which always appalled me. So afraid am I to see it end that I treasure it. Money in one's possession is the instrument of liberty; money one pursues is the instrument of servitude. That is why I hold fast to what I have, but covet no more.'

J-J ROUSSEAU, CONFESSIONS (18th CENTURY)

'He that loveth silver shall not be satisfied with silver, nor he that loveth abundance with increase.'

KOHLETH, 2nd CENTURY AD

The mere possession of money — over and above providing for daily needs, however they are defined — is a form of power; it buys people and time, praise and respect. In the past it bought armies, papal acquiescence, reprieve from punishment, and even the promise of eternal salvation.

A 15th-century Celtic poem 'My purse, gramercy to you for this', attributed to Sion Cent shows us that nothing much has changed in the five centuries since its composition.

> 'My velvet purse, my priest, my coffer of gold, my lord of remedy, my prophet, my dear preserver, you are my mate of the same speech as mine. No better guardian is there under the sky, giver of grave, nest of gold, than you; none better to pay the bills that strangers bring — my purse, gramercy to you for this!
>
> Horses I owned, and honour, jewels and arms, medallions on my shirt, bright gems, a load of rings, chains and brooches ninefold, matchless raiment fit for a well-dressed man, and purpose so to continue, in my land; in Emlyn my would-be kin was numerous — my purse, gramercy to you for this.
>
> . . .
>
> Good is the profit, as Gwenddydd said in verse, good are the things which I have every day, drinks, modish foods, and all provision in commendable guise. I get welcome, and politely called by name, men speak me fair in public, as though bewitched; I get great respect in every market-place, a throne at every banquet in my land, great and long lasting honour done before me — my purse, gramercy to you for this.
>
> If I am taken in manifest theft, red-handed and hauled to course, I know I shall win acquittal when inquest and judgement come upon my case: for forty will swear by perjury, meek enough, on my behalf, three Sundays in succession, and the liberal officers of interrogation all together will be on my side. You are my herald, and my golden coin — my purse, gramercy to you for this.'

TWO CYNICS . . .

THE 18th-CENTURY ESSAYIST, JOSEPH ADDISON

'Gold is a wonderful clearer of the understanding: it dissipates every doubt and scruple in an instant, accommodates itself to the meanest capacities, silences the loud and clamorous, and brings over the most obstinate and inflexible.'

GEORGE BERNARD SHAW, TWO CENTURIES LATER

'Money is the most important thing in the world. It represents health, strength, honour, generosity, and beauty as conspicuously as the want of it represents silliness, weakness, disgrace, meanness and ugliness. Not the least of its virtues is that it destroys base people as certainly as it fortifies and dignifies noble people.'

. . . AND ONE OPTIMIST

THE 18th-CENTURY PHILOSOPHER, EDMUND BURKE

'If we command our wealth we shall be rich and free; if our wealth commands us, we are poor indeed.'

KEEPING IT . . . AND GUARDING IT

Keeping and guarding money — being able to see it, and hear it jingling reassuringly — has always been important.

A form of money box that became popular in the 17th century in northern Europe is the piggy bank. But why a pig? That animal was considered by some to be lucky, and also represented wealth to most rural cottagers. Later examples of money boxes took the form of houses — another visible sign of wealth.

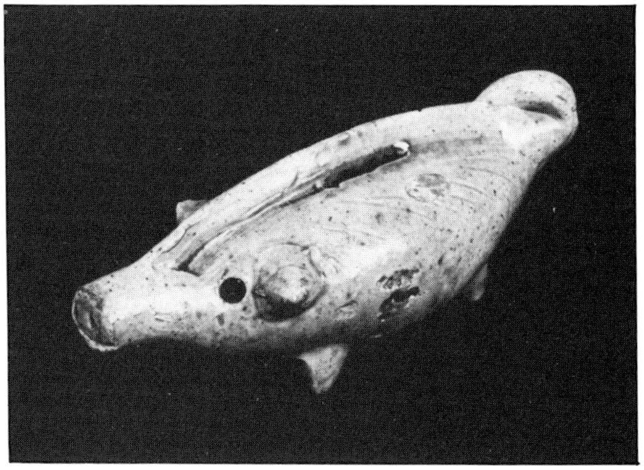

A 17th-century piggy bank.

When mattresses and piggy banks could no longer accommodate accumulated wealth, people turned to other forms of safekeeping. From the United States came one of the most popular solutions: the institutional sa deposit.

One of the best known in London was the Chancery Lane Safe Deposit, opened on 8 May 1885. Journalists were invited to the grand opening, to admire the strong-rooms with two-ton doors, the safety precautions, and the lavishness of its public rooms. Wrought-iron gates, a portcullis, a central marble staircase and handsome archways of red polished granite greeted the depositor. Armed patrol guards watched over the building constantly, and the safe boxes were made of a special material which would not buckle or disintegrate in a fire — one of the main hazards.

An uncanny resemblance — apart from the human hand — to present-day cash dispensing machines.

"I'LL MAKE ASSURANCE DOUBLE SURE" SHAKSPEARE.
EARLY AND PROVIDENT FEAR IS THE MOTHER OF SAFETY.
HAVE YOU HAD QUIET GUARD?
NOT A MOUSE STIRRING.
CHANCERY LANE SAFE DEPOSIT
61 AND 62, CHANCERY LANE. LONDON . W. C.
THE OBJECT OF THE COMPANY IS TO PROVIDE FOR THE USE OF THE PUBLIC AN ABSOLUTELY SECURE BUT INEXPENSIVE DEPOSITORY FOR TITLE DEEDS, JEWELLERY, CASH BOXES, AND VALUABLES OF EVERY DESCRIPTION BY MEANS OF FIRE-PROOF SAFES
EACH RENTER HOLDS THE ONLY KEY OF ACCESS TO HIS OR HER SAFE. VISITORS TO LONDON CAN HAVE THE USE OF THE SAFES FOR SHORT PERIODS. PLATE CHESTS, WILLS, AND OTHER PRIVATE DOCUMENTS TAKEN CHARGE OF IN THE SAFES
THE SAFE DEPOSIT OFFICES AND VAULTS HAVE BEEN CONSTRUCTED UPON THE BEST PRINCIPLES THAT MODERN SCIENCE AND SKILL CAN DEVISE.
"SAFE BIND, SAFE FIND!" A PROVERB NEVER STALE IN THRIFTY MIND. SHAKSPEARE
BY MILNER'S SAFE COMPY LIMITED. LONDON, LIVERPOOL AND MANCHESTER.
EVERY RENTER WILL HAVE ACCESS TO THE VAULT IN WHICH HIS OR HER SAFE IS FIXED AT ALL TIMES DURING BUSINESS HOURS.
THE SAFES ARE GUARDED, DAY AND NIGHT, BY ARMED WATCHMEN.
CONVENIENT WRITING AND WAITING ROOMS FOR THE USE OF RENTERS FREE OF CHARGE
A SEPARATE ROOM BEING PROVIDED FOR THE USE OF LADIES.
CHANCERY LANE SAFE DEPOSIT.
ABSOLUTE SECURITY AND SECRECY
WILLS MAY BE DEPOSITED FOR ONE GUINEA FOR LIFE
ANNUAL RENT OF SAFE ONE TO FIVE GUINEAS
VIEW OF ONE OF THE
STRONG ROOMS FITTED WITH SAFES
ANNUAL RENT OF STRONG ROOMS FIVE TO THIRTY GUINEAS
TRUSTEES AND OTHERS CAN ON APPLICATION HAVE SAFES PROVIDED WITH TWO OR MORE SEPARATE AND DISTINCT KEYS OR COMBINATION LOCKS.
THUS PREVENTING TRUST PROPERTY FROM BEING REMOVED BY ONE TRUSTEE WITHOUT THE KNOWLEDGE OF THE OTHERS. SAFE & SURE.
CASH BOXES GIVEN IN AT NIGHT TO BE RETURNED IN THE MORNING TWO GUINEAS PER ANNUM.
AND SHOP AND OFFICE KEYS TAKEN CHARGE OF AT ONE GUINEA PER ANNUM.
OFFICE HOURS 9.30 AM TO 6. P.M.
SATUR DAYS. 9.30.A.M TO 3.P.M
THE FIRE DEFIED.
MILNER'S PATENT
THE BURGLAR BAFFLED
MILNER'S PATENT
MINERVA GUARDIAN AND PROTECTRESS OF WISDOM ART AND COMMERCE.
MY JEWELLERY IS SECURE
MY DEEDS ARE SAFE
CARDS OF ADMISSION AND PROSPECTUSES MAY BE HAD ON APPLICATION TO THE MANAGER

BANKRUPTCY AND DEBT

Lipuidating old Debts.

'A bankrupt has committed the most dishonourable deed that a man can dishonour his name by being guilty of . . .'

HONORÉ DE BALZAC, CÉSAR BIROTTEAU (1837)

Where money is worshipped and held in high esteem, being in debt or bankrupted is, by contrast, a great evil and gross misdemeanour. For such offences men were sent to jail and treated like hardened criminals. One such prison in the early years of the 19th century consisted of:

'. . . one small courtyard about 19ft square. In addition to the sleeping quarters for men and women, with bare earth flooring, there are two rooms with fireplaces, but no coals are allowed; no saucepans to cook provisions in; no bedsteads, bedding or even straw to lie on. The debtors are obliged to sleep in their clothes upon the dirty boards . . . soap and towels are not provided, so that a man may, for debt of one guinea, remain in this wretched place 40 days without ever taking off his clothes or wash . . . The basic food allowance makes the prisoner, on discharge, fit for hospital, but he is not fit for labour.'

JAMES NEILD, A REPORT ON THE STATE OF IMPRISONED DEBTORS (1801)

But these conditions had persisted for more than a century already. A prisoner at the end of the 17th century — a Mr Morgan, a surgeon from Liverpool — was reduced to so low a state by poverty, neglect and hunger that he was driven to eating mice caught by a cat. When he complained to his jailor he was beaten and put in chains.

Commissioners from a House of Commons investigation committee in 1727 visited Fleet prison and found — among others — a baronet, Sir William Rich, 'in a loathesome dungeon and loaded with irons'.

In their report on the appalling conditions, they declared that some of the torture instruments they were shown 'belonged rather to the dungeons of the Inquisition than to a debtors' prison in the heart of London'.

The prison was closed down in 1844.

THE OLD FLEET PRISON.

There are various gradations of guilt associated with apportioning someone else's money for one's own use. One such 'glossary' has the following permutations:

£1,000,000 — a case of genius
£100,000 — a case of shortage
£50,000 — a case of litigation
£25,000 — a case of insolvency
£10,000 — a case of irregularity
£5,000 — a case of misappropriation
£1,000 — a case of corruption
£500 — a case of embezzlement
£100 — a case of dishonesty
£50 — a case of thievery
£25 — a case of total depravity

AT THE HEAD OF THE PROFESSION.

SCENE—*Prisoners' Waiting-Room adjoining Police Court.* (*Eminently respectable Director awaiting Examination.*)

ARTFUL DODGER (*to* CHARLEY BATES). "YOU'VE BEEN COPPED FOR A TILL—AND ME FOR A CLY. BUT 'E'S BEEN COPPED FOR A BANK—SHARED SOMETHIN' LIKE SIX MILLION SWAG AMONG THE LOT!"

CHARLEY BATES (*in a tone of respectful admiration*). "LOR!"

BUYING FORGIVENESS

To ensure that a man's soul did not rest for ever in Hell, the Church introduced the idea of buying 'indulgencies' — forgiveness. Medieval pardoners appointed by the Church wandered the countryside, dispensing forgiveness granted by Christ and the saints to anyone worried enough to pull out their purse.

Chaucer's pardoner was at least candid:

> **'. . . out come the pence, and specially for myself, for my exclusive purpose is to win and not at all to castigate their sin. Once dead what matters how their souls may fare? They can go blackberrying, for all I care.'**

Death relieves the miser of his "goodies".

But then, alas, falling into the trap of greed, he continues:

> **'. . . do you think, as long as I can preach and get their silver for the things I teach, that I will live in poverty, from choice? No! Let me preach and beg from kirk to kirk and never do an honest job of work, . . . I mean to have money, wool and cheese and wheat, though it were given me by the poorest lad or poorest village widow, though she had a string of starving children. No! let me drink the liquor of the grape and keep a jolly wench in every town.'**

GEOFFREY CHAUCER, CANTERBURY TALES (14th CENTURY)

Burying the dead with sufficient wealth — in the form of gold and silver coins, ornaments and practical utensils — to see them through the trials and tribulations in the unknown afterworld has been a world-wide practice.

We have abandoned this custom. But then burying pound notes with the deceased does not have the same panache as burying a man with all his wealth. Not only would archaeologists in subsequent centuries have less fun; the deceased would have less use of them, we assume, than from the more practical baggage he or she was sent off with in previous centuries.

CHAPTER 6

— THE RICH, THE WEALTHY AND THE MILLIONAIRES —

'I make no claims about the extent of my wealth and I really don't care how rich I am.'

PAUL GETTY

How does one define 'rich'; and is 'millionaire' a word which is worth using as a mark of distinction?

In the US, it is estimated there are over one million millionaires, which means that one in every 250 Americans carries that label. In Britain, the *Sunday Times* recently estimated that there are 20,000 millionaires; of these, around 200 are each worth more than £30 million and seventy are worth more than £100 million.

To be a billionaire may now be the mark of distinction. *Forbes* business magazine listed fourteen such individuals in the US in 1985; in Britain in 1989 there are only nine such individuals or families.

'The capitalist . . . must have fine hearing and a thick skin; must be simultaneously cautious and venturesome, a swashbuckler and a calculator, careless and prudent . . .'

KARL MARX

Really successful men, according to a survey done for *Fortune* magazine some years ago, had distinctive characteristics. They were loners, non-gregarious and detached.

Other included being physically restless, moving about all the time, scratching themselves, drumming their fingers, chain smoking and generally 'twiddling and twitching'.

The circumstances under which these characteristics were observed — in-depth interviews for the magazine — may, of course, have contributed to their very existence.

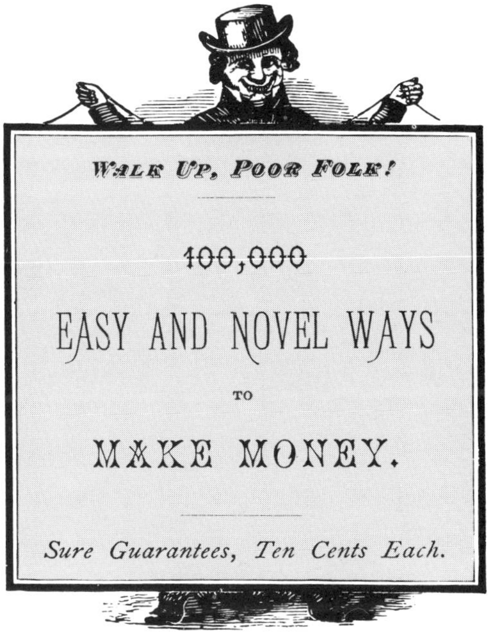

So, how does one gain access to this club?

Some people are born wealthy, some achieve wealth, and others have wealth thrust upon them, even if — as John D. Rockefeller believed — 'God gave me my money'.

> **'I believe the power to make money is a gift of God,' he once admitted, 'to be developed and used to the best of our ability for the good of mankind. Having been endowed with the gift I possess, I believe it is my duty to make money and still more money, and to use the money I make for the good of my fellow men according to the dictates of my conscience.'**

As a schoolboy, John D. Rockefeller announced to a friend, as they walked past a rich man's sumptuous house: 'when I grow up I want to be worth $100,000'. He underestimated himself. By the turn of the century he was in fact 'worth a billion.

'Money is the seed of money, and the first guinea is sometimes more difficult to acquire than the second million.'

•JEAN-JACQUES ROUSSEAU, 18th CENTURY

'The way to wealth, if you desire it, is as plain as the way to market. It depends chiefly on two words, industry and frugality; that is, waste neither time nor money, but make the best use of both.'

BENJAMIN FRANKLIN

'It is not abundance that maketh rich, but Economy.'

ANON

In the opinion of the pragmatic 15th-century architect and painter Leone Battista Alberti, the five routes to success and wealth were:

1. Wholesale trade;
2. Seeking (and presumably finding) a treasure trove;
3. Ingratiating oneself with a rich man and becoming his heir;
4. Usury;
5. Rental of pastures, horses and the like.

'The secret of success? Never tell any one what you are going to do till you've done it . . . and bide your time.'

CORNELIUS VANDERBILT, 19th CENTURY

Paul Getty believed that wealth came through one's own efforts — with a little bit of luck thrown in:

> 'Luck, knowledge, hard work — especially hard work — a man needs them all to become a millionaire.'

Getty made his first billion — by his own account — in the Great Oil Rush of the early 20th century. The roads to riches were not paved with gold; but 'unpaved — rivers of mushy clay and mud in spring and winter, and sun-baked, rutted tracks perpetually shrouded by billowing clouds of harsh red or yellow dust in summer.' Looking back on his successes, he later mused:

> **'Believe me, wealth is something with which one has to learn to live — and the task is not always as simple as might be imagined . . .**
>
> **In some ways a millionaire just can't win. If he spends too freely, he is criticised for being extravagant and ostentatious. If on the other hand, he lives quietly and thriftily, the same people who would have criticised him for being profligate will call him a miser. If he goes to parties and night clubs, he is labelled a wastrel and doubts are raised about his maturity and sense of responsibility. Let him shun the salons and saloons, and he is promptly tagged as a recluse or misanthrope.'**

One simple way of not squandering his wealth involved the practical solution of installing pay telephones for his guests in his English country home, Sutton Place, in the Surrey countryside.

An article in *Fortune* magazine in 1957 labelled Getty 'the richest man in America'. Fifty years earlier, it was Andrew Carnegie who was congratulated by J. Pierpoint Morgan on becoming 'the richest man in the world' on selling his interests in the US Steel Corporation to Morgan. The personal fortune that earned him that title was estimated to be $313 million.

Carnegie's 'Gospel of Wealth', propounded in 1889 when he was 54:

> **'This, then, is held to be the duty of a man of wealth: to set an example of modest, unostentatious living, shunning display or extravagance; to provide moderately for the legitimate wants of those dependent on him; and after doing so, to consider all surplus revenues which come to him simply as trust funds which he is called upon to administer, and strictly bound as a matter of duty to administer in the manner which, in his judgement, is best calculated to provide the most beneficial results for the community -- the man of wealth thus becoming the mere trustee and agent for his poorer brethren.'**

For Aristotle Onassis, the Greek shipping magnate, the route to success was of a more Mediterranean, sybaritic nature. Just five years before his death, he shared his ten 'secrets for success':

1. Take care of your body. Make yourself as good as you can. Don't worry about shortcomings. Look at me. I am no Greek god but I did not waste my life in crying because I wasn't born good looking. Remember nobody is as ugly as he thinks he is.

2. Eat lightly and stay away from the wines and rich food when you have a job to do. Spending several hours at the table in the middle of a working day is the best way to shorten your life.

3. Wait until evening, when you have more time and the day's labour is finished. Then enjoy a good meal with friends, and never talk business while you eat.

4. Exercise and keep yourself trim. The basic yoga exercises help immensely, both mind and body. And if you can manage an hour or two of judo every week, it frees you of all your complexes.

5. Keep a tan even if you have to use a lamp. To most people a tan in winter means only that you have been where the sun is, and in that respect, sun is money.

6. Once you have taken care of your physical appearance, establish a successful way of life. Live in an elegant building — even if you have to take a room in the attic — where you will rub shoulders with wealthy, successful people in the corridors and on the elevators. Frequent luxury cafés even if you have to sip your drinks. Soon you will learn that many people with money are very lonely.

7. If you are short of money, borrow it. And never ask for small loans. Borrow big but always repay promptly.

8. Keep your troubles to yourself and let people believe you are having a wonderful time.

9. Don't sleep too much or you'll wake up a failure. If you sleep three hours less each night for a year, you will have an extra month and a half to succeed in.

10. If you aspire for success, do not squander your time reading about things others have done. It is better to get on living your own life than to concern yourself with what others have done.

His daughter Christina, born to immense riches and later to inherit the entire Onassis wealth, once said:

'Money doesn't bring happiness — I know.'

In addition to either inheriting wealth, or working hard to achieve it, there is also the possibility of marrying into it.

Ogden Nash considered this, but came to the conclusion that:

'The rich marry only the rich.
It is one of our national disasters
That, broadly speaking, Astors and Vanderbilts and
Rockefellers and Morgans never marry anybody but
Morgans and Rockefellers and Vanderbilts and Astors,
Whereas if they only bestowed their affections on somebody
in a lower crust,
Why money would be distributed over this broad land of
ours like dust,
So I think they may all be rich but honest,
But I think their matchmaking proclivities ought to be
harnessed.
Yes, if money marrying money were prohibited,
How speedily and how painlessly it would be redistributed.
Yes, yes, the rich and the poor can settle and forget their
differences just as the Blue and the Gray have
As soon as we have a law saying that people can only marry
people who have a lot less money than they have . . .'

OGDEN NASH, SONG OF SONGS (20th CENTURY)

Money could, however, also buy rich American heiresses an aristocratic title. It has been estimated that more than 500 such 'dollar princesses' married into European nobility at the turn of the 20th century, bringing with them more than $200 million to help restore the crumbling fortunes and mansions of their new spouses.

Asked how he came by his riches (estimated between $700 million and $1 billion), Malcolm Forbes, owner of America's *Forbes* business magazine and source of the annual listing of America's richest people, replied:

'Through sheer ability, spelt i-n-h-e-r-i-t-a-n-c-e.'

OLD MONEY . . . NEW MONEY

Cornelius Vanderbilt IV once defined old money as 'aged in the wood' money, fortunes accumulated from tobacco and cotton, railroads and banking, long before Gettysburg in 1863.

Old money lived around Fifth Avenue in New York, had summer retreats on Long Island, and kept their money in government bonds or cash.

New money was accumulated in the mills of Pittsburgh, the mountains of Montana, and the mines of California.

New money settled on Park Avenue, and spent unwisely on furs and the French Riviera. New money's status symbols *par excellence* were the yacht and the Pullman coach.

William Randolph Hearst's mother in conversation with financier Russell Sage:

> Sage: If your son continues to attack the institutions of Wall Street, he will lose one million dollars a year.
>
> Mrs Hearst: At that rate he can stay in business another 80 years.

Definition of 'genius' and 'capital':

> 'Mr Longfellow can take a worthless sheet of paper, and by writing a poem on it, make it worth 50 dollars — that's genius. Vanderbilt can write fewer words on a much smaller sheet, and make it worth 50,000,000 dollars — that's capital.'

◆

THORSTEIN VEBLEN, THEORY OF THE LEISURE CLASSES (1899)

> '. . . as fast as a person makes new acquisitions and becomes accustomed to the resulting new standard of wealth, the standard forthwith ceases to afford appreciably greater satisfaction than the old standard did . . . The tendency is constantly to make the present pecuniary standard the point of departure for the fresh increase of wealth.'

As always, the rich and successful elicit both admiration and contempt in others. Charles Francis Adams, brother of philosopher Henry, who knew the American business and financial giants at the turn of the 20th century, wrote of them:

> 'As I approach the end, I am more than a little puzzled to account for the instances I have seen of business success — money-getting. It comes from rather a low instinct. Certainly so far as my observation goes, it is scarcely met with in combination with the finer or more interesting traits of character. I have known, and known tolerably well, a great many 'successful' men — 'big' financially — men famous during the last half century, and a less interesting crowd I do not care to encounter. Not one that I have ever known would I care to meet again either in this world or the next; nor is one associated in my mind with the idea of humour, thought or refinement. As a set of mere money-getters and traders, they were essentially unattractive.'

Nevertheless, Russell H. Conwell, pastor and founder of Temple University in Pennsylvania, uncompromisingly urged his students to make money: 'to make money honestly is to preach the gospel'.

> 'Let me say here clearly,' he continued, 'ninety-eight out of one hundred of the rich men of America are honest. That is why they are rich. That is why they are trusted with money. That is why they carry on great enterprises and find plenty of people to work with them. It is because they are honest men.'

Duroy, Guy de Maupassant's cynical social climber, was not so sure, and showed contempt for those he nevertheless strove to emulate.

"Duroy walked slowly, drinking in the fresh air which tasted as delicious as fresh bread. He went past the Arc de Triomphe and started walking along the main avenue in the opposite direction to the riders. He watched them as they trotted or galloped, men and women, the rich ones of the world, and now he found himself barely envying them. He knew almost all of them by name, the state of their finances and their secret lives, since his duties had made him a sort of Who's Who for all the celebrities of Paris — and for their scandals . . .

He saw quite a number who were suspected of cheating at cards, or who in many cases used gambling clubs as their major source of income, certainly a dubious one.

There were others, with famous names, who lived entirely on their wives' private incomes, as everyone well knew; others who lived similarly on their mistresses', as everyone suspected. Many had paid their debts (an honourable action) without anybody's ever discovering where they had found the money (a much less honourable secret). He saw financiers whose immense wealth was based on robbery, but who were welcome everywhere, in the noblest houses, and also men so respected that ordinary people raised their hats to them as they passed but whose scandalous speculation in state-controlled enterprises was perfectly familiar to all those who knew the shady things that take place behind the scenes.

All of them were haughty, with a sneer on their lips, an insolent look in their eyes, men with side whiskers and men with moustaches."

Duroy was laughing to himself as he repeated:
"What a set, the whole filthy bunch of crooks!"

GUY DE MAUPASSANT, BEL AMI (1885)

HONESTY HAS ITS REWARDS

A contemporary writer had this to say of the banker J. Pierpoint Morgan:

> 'Wall Street and Lombard Street both spoke of him with bated breath. His schemes for multiplying ordinary fortunes into colossal accumulations of wealth made him appear to the small fry of finance as a modern Midas whose magic touch turned everything to gold . . . He asserted an irresistible influence over all he met, and he justified their belief in him by the inviolability of his plighted work.'

Integrity and honouring one's word were to him vital elements for success, and he expected those qualities in people with whom he did business.

During his questioning by Attorney Samuel Untermeyer in the hearings on the 'Money Trust Investigation' (1912) — where the contention was that a small handful of men controlled the vast resources of the US, and acted as a group of 'voracious spiders', J. P. Morgan offered an insight on how he, as a banker, assessed his fellow men:

Untermeyer: The control of credit involves a control of money, does it not?

JP: *A control of credit? No. . . .*

Untermeyer: But the basis of banking is credit, is it not?

JP: *Not always. That is an evidence of banking, but it is not the money itself. Money is gold, and nothing else . . .*

Untermeyer: Is not the credit based upon money?

JP: *No, sir . . . I know lots of men, business men who can borrow any amount, whose credit is unquestioned.*

Untermeyer: Is that not because it is believed that they have the money back of them?

JP: *No, sir; it is because people believe in the man.*

Untermeyer: And it is regardless of whether he has any financial backing at all, is it?

JP: *It is very often.*

Untermeyer: And he might not be worth anything?

JP: *He might not have anything. I have known a man to come into my office, and I have given him a check for a million dollars when I knew he had not a cent in the world . . .*

Untermeyer: Is not commercial credit based primarily on money or property?

JP: *No, sir; the first thing is character.*

Untermeyer: Before money or property?

JP: *Before money, or anything else. Money cannot buy it . . . a man I do not trust could not get money from me for all the bonds in Christendom.*

. . . Untermeyer then asked him whether this was the way money was loaned generally on Wall Street.

JP: *That is the way I loan it.*

Honesty was a quality expected even of the general public, as advertisements in a London news-sheet of 1782 indicates.

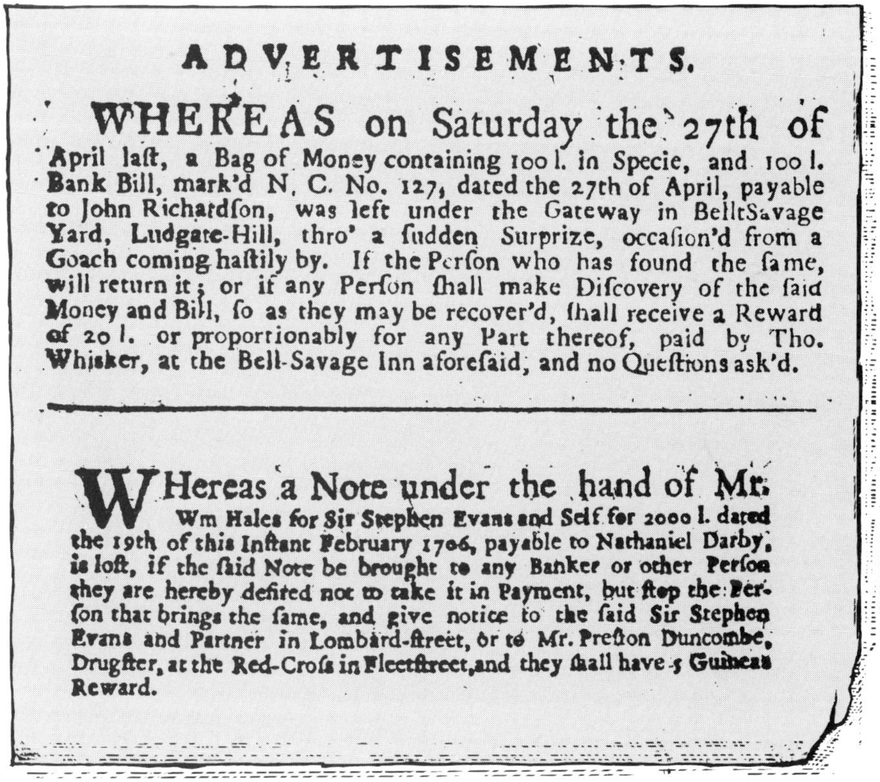

ADVERTISEMENTS.

WHEREAS on Saturday the 27th of April laſt, a Bag of Money containing 100 l. in Specie, and 100 l. Bank Bill, mark'd N. C. No. 127, dated the 27th of April, payable to John Richardſon, was left under the Gateway in BellSavage Yard, Ludgate-Hill, thro' a ſudden Surprize, occaſion'd from a Coach coming haſtily by. If the Perſon who has found the ſame, will return it; or if any Perſon ſhall make Diſcovery of the ſaid Money and Bill, ſo as they may be recover'd, ſhall receive a Reward of 20 l. or proportionably for any Part thereof, paid by Tho. Whisker, at the Bell-Savage Inn aforeſaid; and no Queſtions ask'd.

WHereas a Note under the hand of Mr. Wm Hales for Sir Stephen Evans and Self for 2000 l. dated the 19th of this Inſtant February 1706, payable to Nathaniel Darby, is loſt, if the ſaid Note be brought to any Banker or other Perſon they are hereby deſired not to take it in Payment, but ſtop the Perſon that brings the ſame, and give notice to the ſaid Sir Stephen Evans and Partner in Lombard-ſtreet, or to Mr. Preſton Duncombe, Drugſter, at the Red-Croſs in Fleetſtreet, and they ſhall have 5 Guineas Reward.

THE ROTHSCHILD INSTINCT

The Rothschilds, on the other hand, were credited with 'a remarkable instinct which causes them always to choose right. Their enormous wealth (they are the richest people in Europe) is entirely a result of this instinct'.

But this instinct was blended with organisational ability: legends abound about how Nathan Rothschild received news about the Battle of Waterloo a full twenty-four hours before the British Government. The reality was simple: a remarkably efficient courier service linking the Rothschild Amsterdam offices with the battlefield, messengers with fresh post horses, and knowledge of ships sailing across the Channel.

NATHAN ROTHSCHILD

It was on the strength of this knowledge that Rothschild invested heavily in government stock before its value rose the next day on the news of Wellington's victory, giving Rothschild a considerable profit — and earning him an immortal reputation.

His other strength was diplomacy: the ability to keep on good terms with whoever was in power — of whatever political complexion — not always easy for a Jewish banker among Gentiles. As the philosopher and writer Heine put it: 'Money is the God of our time, and Rothschild is his prophet'.

His portly figure would be seen propping up one of the pillars of the Exchange — always the same one, in the corner reserved for Jews not licensed as brokers. When he was prevented, one day, from taking up his usual position, it created a stir on the Exchange.

> 'It requires a great deal of boldness, and a great deal of caution to make a great fortune; and when you have got it, it requires ten times as much wit to keep it.'
>
> *ROTHSCHILD*

FORTUNE AND FABULIST

A Writer of Fables was passing through a lonely forest, when he met a Fortune. Greatly alarmed, he tried to climb a tree, but the Fortune pulled him down and bestowed itself upon him with cruel persistence.

'Why do you try to run away?' said the Fortune, when his struggles had ceased and his screams were stifled. 'Why do you glare at me so inhospitably?'

'I don't know what you are,' replied the Writer of Fables, deeply disturbed.

'I am wealth; I am respectability,' the Fortune explained; 'I am elegant houses, a yacht and a clean shirt every day. I am leisure, I am travel, wine, a shiny hat and an unshiny coat. I am enough to eat.'

'All right,' said the Writer of Fables, in a whisper; 'but for goodness' sake speak lower!'

'Why so?' the Fortune asked, in surprise.

'So as not to wake me,' replied the Writer of Fables, a holy calm brooding upon his beautiful face.

AMBROSE BIERCE, EARLY 20th CENTURY

Of course, there are always those whom luck favours. As La Bruyère, the 17th-century French writer put it:

'. . . stupid men and I dare even say imbeciles, who find themselves good places and are able to die rich without one having any reason to suspect that they have contributed to this by their labour or the slightest industry; someone simply took them to the source of a river, or perhaps mere chance put them in its way; they were asked 'Do you want water? Take it. And they took it.'

'Money hides a thousand deformities.'

CHINESE PROVERB

TWO RENAISSANCE BILLIONAIRES

Jacques Coeur, dubbed a 15th-century tycoon, had two rules for success: keeping his options open, and diversifying.

He made his initial money by trading in luxury goods with the Levant. He then diversified into mining of copper, shipping and banking, to all of which he brought, for those days, a sound 'business' education. He traded successfully in everything: money and arms, peltry and jewellery, brocades and woollens, 'the seas being covered with his ships'. He was a banker, a broker and a farmer. To this he added the post of Master of the Mint, and later steward of the royal expenditure. He made advances to his king, Charles VII, in his wars against the English, and lent to needy courtiers, and members of the royal family — thus creating a vast network of jealous debtors, and a widely held belief that he had discovered the secret of the philosopher's stone.

This — and the poisoning of the king's mistress Agnes Sorel (of which some suspected him) — proved to be his downfall. Tried by his peers and judges — many of whom were also his debtors — he was thrown into prison; and escaped only to die a few years later.

Jacob Fugger the Rich, of Augsburg, had a somewhat different recipe for success — with an ingredient which could lead to difficulties, as several of his banking predecessors had found — lending to monarchs, but from a position of strength: ownership of major silver and copper mines. He combined this with a meticulous attention to accounting details (having learnt double-entry book-keeping as a young man in Venice), and a serious business-like approach to all his affairs.

The relationship between this 16th-century Augsburg merchant banker and his clientele of kings and princes — and in particular Charles V — was a symbiotic one: each needed the other. The protection and privileges accorded by the latter gave Jacob Fugger the means to offer them the one major ingredient they lacked: money.

Born into an already wealthy merchant family, he proceeded to make it fabulously rich. His loans to kings and princes, backed up by ownership of the best and largest silver and copper mines in Hungary, Bohemia and the Tyrol, rested on a flourishing and expanding merchant business at the cross-roads of Europe.

Jacob Fugger lent the vast sums needed to back the Emperor Maximillian — and bribe the Electors — in his quest to have his grandson Charles V crowned Holy Roman Emperor in 1519.

And the Fuggers were the Papal 'salesmen' — conveying indulgences and benefices (payments for appointments to bishoprics and other holy offices) through their network across Europe back to Rome. Martin Luther was horrified that '. . . this citizen of Augsburg can collect three tons of gold in an hour, which is more than the kings of France and England can do'.

GILBART'S WORKS, A PRACTICAL TREATISE ON BANKING (1865)

'In ancient Rome the merchants and bankers had a public procession each year to the Temple of Mercury — who, by a strange association, was regarded as the god of merchants and of bankers, of thieves, and of eloquence — to offer sacrifices for the blessings they had received; and, as the satirists said, to ask forgiveness for all the frauds and tricks they had practiced in their trade during the past year.'

And then there is the possibility of gaining your fortune through the misfortunes of others.

One character who gained his initial wealth through fire was the 1st-century BC Roman — and contemporary of Julius Caesar — Marcus Licinius Crassus.

He gained his money, literally, by fire. Taking advantage of there being no town fire brigade in Rome, he organised his own, and when houses — and soon whole neighbourhoods — were ablaze, he would arrive and bargain with the horrified owners what price they would pay for his help. If too little was offered, the conflagration continued.

His next acquisitions were properties belonging to the followers of the 'revolutionary' Marius. Thereafter he turned his hand to schooling slaves and making his next fortune. His end, however, was ignominious, but befitting of his life: he was beheaded and, it is said, his head filled with molten gold.

CHAPTER 7

— THE POWER OF MONEY —

'The use of money is all the advantage there is in having money.'

BENJAMIN FRANKLIN, 18th CENTURY

We spend our money to give ourselves pleasure, and to enhance our standing in other people's eyes.

Feasting has always been a way of displaying wealth.

At one banquet held at the Court of Burgundy in 1454, eight and twenty musicians emerged from a pie; other feasts of the period produced dwarfs from mock castles, and jugglers and acrobats leaping from vast puddings.

A near neighbour, in Champagne country, the Duc de Berri, added to these pleasures by dining off gold plate, using silver forks and spoons of cornelian and serpentine (individual forks made their appearance in Venice in the 15th century — to be condemned as a 'diabolical luxury' by one German preacher).

The City of London fathers — in time-honoured fashion — lavished money on 'a feast unparalleled in history for its magnificence' in 1641 for their doomed monarch, Charles I. The meal itself consisted of 500 dishes, and as part of the reception, various guilds tested out their inventiveness: the Goldsmiths built a square tower in Cheapside from which flowed a permanent stream of wine; the Grocers created a tropical island of exotic spices and fruits, and the Skinners erected a forest full of wild beasts.

Just over two hundred years later they again regaled the reigning monarch, George III, with a hospitality which cost them £6,878.5s.4d. The centre spread caught the attention particularly, created of '32 Cold Things of Sorts, viz Temples, Shapes, and landscapes of Jellies, Savory cakes and Almond Gothes', and 'a Grand Pyramid of Shellfish'. All this, after the king had feasted himself on quail, teal, pheasant, partridge, Westphalian hams, fat livers, eggs and green truffles.

A feast in preparation.

Gourmet palates were tempted in 16th-century Italy by such delicacies as marzipan from Siena, sausages from Bologna, gnocchi with garlic from Piacenza, fish and oysters from Venice, and an excellent bread from Padua.

In the early 1700s, rich Parisians scorned goats cheese in favour of Roquefort, Parmesan and Sassenage from the Dauphine. Some decades later the fashionable Parisian was prepared to eat butter from two regions of France only, scorning that from Britanny and Ireland. At the same time he was being urged to 'taste the wines of Romanée, Saint Vivant, Citeaux and Graves . . . but best of all insist on Tokay if you meet it . . . it is the greatest wine in the world and only the masters of the world should drink it'.

The great chef, Escoffier, the creator of dishes named after wealthy patrons — such as pêche Melba — whose flamboyant meals delighted the palates of the rich at the Ritz in Paris at the turn of the century, has his followers in the *nouvelle cuisine* and *cuisine naturelle* creators who content the current cognoscenti with minute but beautifully presented slivers of food. (Even they had their precursors: in 1768 one gourmet was writing: 'the new cooking is all juice and jelly'.)

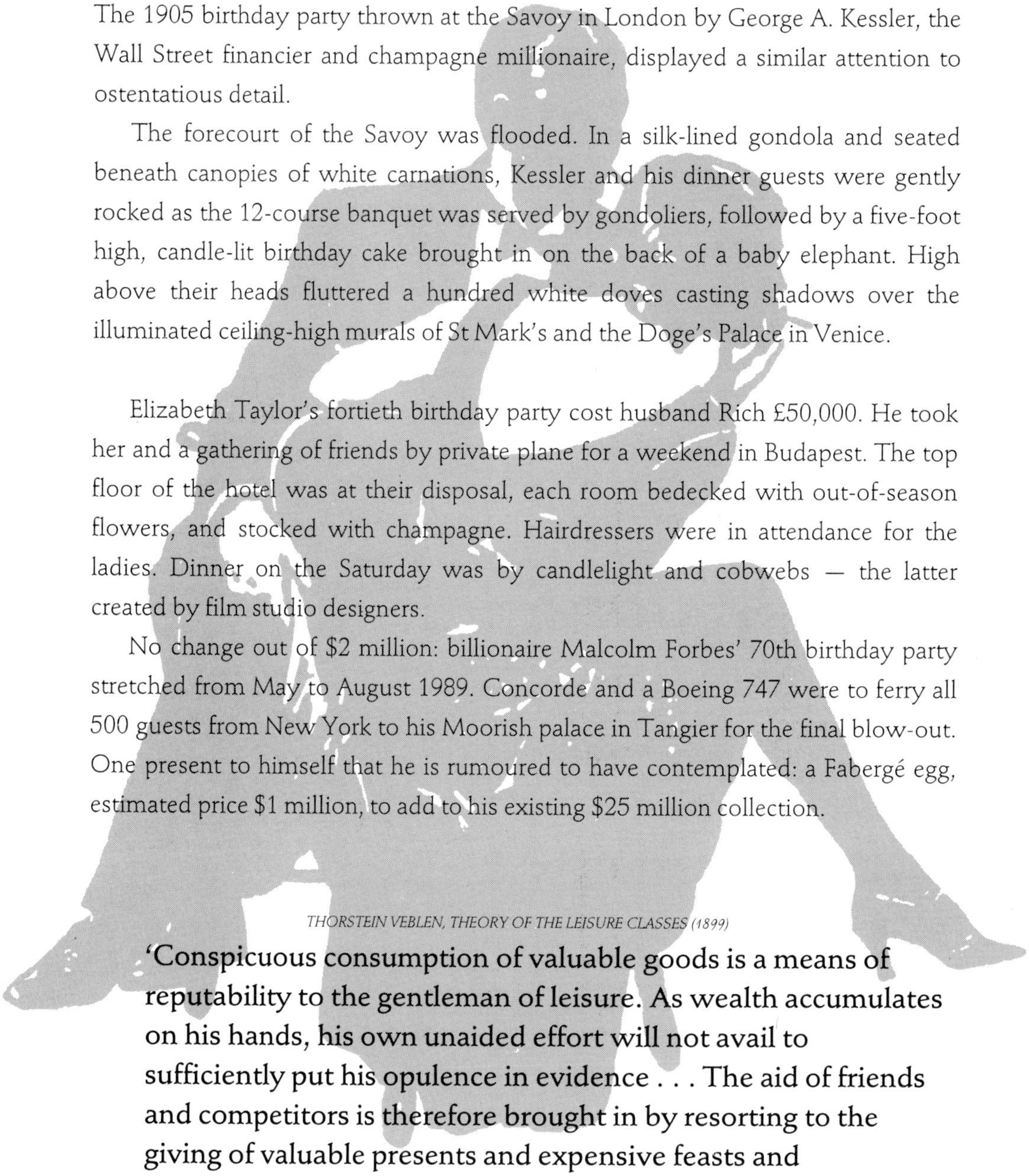

The 1905 birthday party thrown at the Savoy in London by George A. Kessler, the Wall Street financier and champagne millionaire, displayed a similar attention to ostentatious detail.

The forecourt of the Savoy was flooded. In a silk-lined gondola and seated beneath canopies of white carnations, Kessler and his dinner guests were gently rocked as the 12-course banquet was served by gondoliers, followed by a five-foot high, candle-lit birthday cake brought in on the back of a baby elephant. High above their heads fluttered a hundred white doves casting shadows over the illuminated ceiling-high murals of St Mark's and the Doge's Palace in Venice.

Elizabeth Taylor's fortieth birthday party cost husband Rich £50,000. He took her and a gathering of friends by private plane for a weekend in Budapest. The top floor of the hotel was at their disposal, each room bedecked with out-of-season flowers, and stocked with champagne. Hairdressers were in attendance for the ladies. Dinner on the Saturday was by candlelight and cobwebs — the latter created by film studio designers.

No change out of $2 million: billionaire Malcolm Forbes' 70th birthday party stretched from May to August 1989. Concorde and a Boeing 747 were to ferry all 500 guests from New York to his Moorish palace in Tangier for the final blow-out. One present to himself that he is rumoured to have contemplated: a Fabergé egg, estimated price $1 million, to add to his existing $25 million collection.

THORSTEIN VEBLEN, THEORY OF THE LEISURE CLASSES (1899)

'Conspicuous consumption of valuable goods is a means of reputability to the gentleman of leisure. As wealth accumulates on his hands, his own unaided effort will not avail to sufficiently put his opulence in evidence . . . The aid of friends and competitors is therefore brought in by resorting to the giving of valuable presents and expensive feasts and entertainment . . .'

Duc Jean Floressas des Esseintes in Huysman's novel, *Against Nature,* a dandy and aesthete modelled on the young Baudelaire:

'. . . won a considerable reputation as an eccentric — a reputation which he crowned by wearing suits of white velvet with gold-laced waistcoats, by sticking a bunch of Parma violets in his shirt-front in lieu of a cravat and by entertaining men of letters to dinners . . . One of these meals, modelled on an eighteenth-century original, had been a funeral feast to mark the most ludicrous of personal misfortunes.

The dining room, draped in black, opened onto a garden metamorphosed for the occasion, the paths being strewn with charcoal, the ornamental pond edged with black basalt and filled with ink, and the shrubberies replaced with cypresses and pines. The dinner itself was served on a black cloth adorned with baskets of violets and scabious; candelabra shed an eerie green light over the table . . .

While a hidden orchestra played funeral marches, the guests were waited on by naked negresses wearing only slippers and stockings in cloth of silver embroidered with tears.

Dining off black-bordered plates, the company had enjoyed turtle soup, Russian rye bread, ripe olives from Turkey, caviar, mullet botargo, black puddings from Frankfurt, game served in sauces the colour of liquorice and boot-polish, truffles and jellies, chocolate creams; plum puddings, nectarines, pears in grape-juice syrup; mulberries, and black heart-cherries. From dark-tinted glasses they had drunk the wines of Limagne and Roussillon, of Tenedos, Valdepenas and Oporto. And after coffee and walnut cordial, they had rounded off the evening with kvass, porter and stout.

On the invitations, which were similar to those sent out before more solemn obsequies, this dinner was described as a funeral banquet in memory of the host's virility, lately but only temporarily deceased.'

J-K HUYSMANS, AGAINST NATURE (1884)

DAILY LUXURIES AND SUMPTUARY LAWS

'. . . expensive living . . . is a kind of slow fever . . . a secret enemy that feeds upon the vitals . . .'

DANIEL DEFOE, 18th CENTURY

Sumptuary laws, introduced to prevent conspicuous consumption in times of economic difficulty, were invoked by most European rulers and governments at one time or another from medieval to modern times. Although intended ostensibly to prevent waste, it has been claimed that the avaricious sumptuary laws were initiated in a spirit of resentment by the old noble families against the imitations and spending of the *nouveaux riches*. In fact, although these laws pinpointed lavish spending, they were powerless to prevent it. Their attempted iron fist tended to fall on two of man's greatest means of advertising his wealth: his food and his clothing.

In 1461, the Senate in Venice forbade banquets costing more than a ducat per head, and banned such meats as peacock, pheasant and partridge.

Similar laws were being passed in Amsterdam in the mid-17th century against 'unnecessary and sumptuous banquets', including limiting the number of musicians to six.

In 14th-century Tuscany, Francesco Datini, the merchant from Prato whose letters and papers have given us such an insight into daily life in his time, managed to circumvent the sumptuary laws which limited the number of people allowed to gather at any celebration. This might have affected the wedding feast of his daughter, but since every guest was allowed — by law — to bring a companion, there was no problem.

The wedding banquet was limited, theoretically, to three courses: the first of 'pasta' dishes, the second 'a roast with pie', and the third, a blancmange. The pie provided one escape route to avoid the guests leaving hungry: it ingeniously consisted of pork, chicken, ham, eggs, dates, almonds, flour, spices, saffron, sugar and salt. No limit was placed on how much food could be piled onto a guest's plate, with the result that a seven-pound capon, or a goose, could happily be offered to each visitor.

In Roman times, under Trajan, conspicuous consumption was closely linked to bribery. Pliny described how the Senate had decided that 'candidates [to the senate] should be prohibited from providing entertainments, distributing presents and depositing money with agents'. And for a brief period during Cicero's life a sumptuary law limited the amount of meat which could be eaten.

Clothing, and particularly women's clothing, was also the subject of sumptuary laws. At one time in Venice, real pearls were not to be worn on gowns. In Florence, multicoloured, striped, checked or embossed velvets and silks were forbidden, as were brocade, samite and rich embroideries in silver and gold. Long trains which used up a great deal of material, and cloak fur linings of ermine were likewise prohibited (except to magistrates, doctors and knights); but those made of squirrel or cat and lined further with bright coloured taffeta were acceptable. Finally, the number of buttons on a garment had to be limited and they could only be placed between the wrist and the elbow.

Henri IV and his nobles were upset to find silk being worn by the *nouveaux riches* merchants of 16th-century Paris, and the king decreed that this should not be so. Nevertheless, the Venetian ambassador to Henri's court commented: 'a man . . . is not considered rich unless he has twenty-five to thirty suits of different types, and he must change them every day'.

'A single man in possession of a good fortune must be in want of a wife.'

JANE AUSTEN, 18th CENTURY

DREAM CASTLES . . . AND COTTAGES

At the turn of this century, wealthy Americans of the East Coast — many of them filled with the wonders of their first taste of Europe — built their dream castles and 'cottages' on the strip of land at Newport, Rhode Island, overlooking the Atlantic Ocean.

'A Vanderbilt cottage', Newport, Rhode Island.

— The Belmonts (he was Rothschild's representative in New York) built themselves a $3 million 'cottage', Belcourt Castle, which they shared with thirty horses, housed on the ground floor. Each night the horses were wrapped in white initialled Irish linen sheets and covered by blankets embroidered with the Belmont coat of arms. Alva Belmont was also the first proud owner of a French motor car in Newport.

— Cornelius Vanderbilt II built his 'cottage', The Breakers — 'a 70-room mausoleum' — at a total cost of $10 million; $5,000 was needed annually to maintain the perimeter fence.

On the West coast, above the rolling blue Pacific, William Randolph Hearst, newspaper publisher and financier of the growing film industry in Hollywood, constructed his dream on a hillside. Filled with antiques and treasures on which he spent part of his vast fortune, San Simeon — a mixture of medieval grandeur and classical pastiche — stood in grounds of over 250,000 acres.

The dining room, Cardiff Castle.

On a more modest scale, but equally flamboyant, the 3rd Marquess of Bute, who inherited his father's wealth — made from financing much of the building of the Cardiff docks in the earlier part of the 19th century — engaged William Burges to create his dream: a romantic Camelot. His chosen site was the part-derelict Cardiff Castle. Within it he created a vast Gothic fantasy from tiles, mosaics, silk wallpapers, and vaulted ceilings embossed with gold.

Carried away on a Wagnerian dream of Teutonic tales, the fabulously wealthy Ludwig of Bavaria created his own fantasy fairy-tale castle of Neuschwanstein, to complement his other two castles: Linderhof, with its moorish extravagance, and the Versailles-like opulence of Herrenchiemsee.

The Rothschild banking family of Frankfurt settled in England, and by the early 19th century had assumed the life-style of the rich in their adopted country, with City offices, country houses, sporting acclaims and parliamentary aspirations.

Mayer Amschel was the first of the family to build in the Buckinghamshire countryside. In Mentmore, he created a treasure trove:

> **'It was like fairyland when I entered the great palace, and got at once into the great hall', wrote Lady Eastlake in 1872. 'Forty feet by fifty, and about one hundred feet high, hung with tapestries, floored with parquet and Persian carpets; an open arcade runs round and looks down through arches into the hall, which is filled with gorgeous masses of flowers and every sumptuous object that wealth can command. From this great centre hall branch off lobbies floored with white marble; then three splendid drawing rooms, two libraries, billiard room — every place almost crammed with precious articles in enamel, bronze, gold, silver, amber, jewels etc.**
>
> **. . . I don't believe the Medicis were so lodged in the height of their glory!'**

The homes of his cousin Ferdinand and his brother Alfred met with less approval. Staying in the former home, Mary Gladstone felt 'much oppressed with the extreme gorgeousness and luxury'. Of the latter, Eustace Balfour wrote: 'I have never seen anything more terribly vulgar . . . outside it is a combination of a French château and a gambling house. Inside it is badly planned . . . and gaudily decorated. Oh, the hideousness of everything, the showiness. The sense of lavish wealth thrust up your nose!'

The taste of the wealthy has always been closely scrutinised, particularly when it belonged to the *nouveaux riches*.

Aristotle Onassis' yacht, the *Christina* — a 'rich man's toy' — had so many gadgets that every part of the ship was crammed with electronic equipment to provide maximum luxury: a vast air-conditioning plant was squeezed in between decks; a sophisticated alarm system was triggered off by open portholes or a sharp rise in temperature; and the sea water in the outdoor swimming pool was kept a few degrees below air temperature so guests would feel pleasantly refreshed when they dived in. To meet Onassis' wish to have somewhere to dance on the main deck, his architect managed to design the bottom of the pool — decorated with mosaic scenes from Greek mythology — to be lifted electronically to the level of the deck to provide a dance floor.

No expense was spared when song-writer Cole Porter's wife decided to decorate her living rooms with platinum wallpaper, cover her floors with zebra-skin carpets, and have red laquered chairs upholstered with white kid . . . somewhat reminiscent of Eartha Kitt's immortally sung words:

'I'm just an old-fashioned girl with an old-fashioned mind . . . Instead of fitted carpets, I'll have money wall to wall . . .'

JEWELLERY

Jewellery has always been a symbol of wealth. Louis XIV is said to have owned a diamond-covered coat worth 14 million francs — sumptuous even by Versailles standards.

Two women this century have stood out with their love for flamboyant jewellery — Mrs Simpson (the Duchess of Windsor) and Elizabeth Taylor.

Elizabeth Taylor's love of jewels has been legendary. It is thought that at one time she owned $8 million-worth. Among her historic pieces was a pearl once owned by Queen Mary I of England — a present from her husband, Philip II of Spain — and a heart-shaped pendant that once belonged to Shah Jehan, who built the Taj Mahal in memory of his beloved wife. Her most famous acquisition was one of the world's largest cut diamonds, priced at over $1 million, given to her by Richard Burton on their yacht, the *Kalizma*; a plaque still marks the spot.

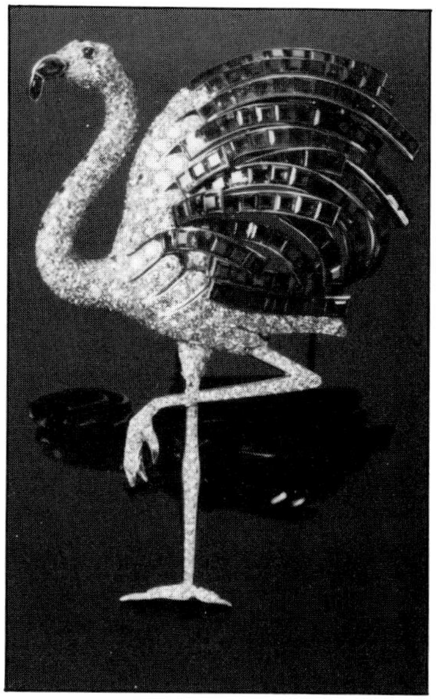

A ruby, sapphire, emerald, citrine and diamond clip in the shape of a flamingo, mounted by Cartier for the Duchess of Windsor in 1940.

The *Times* of the day commented:

> **'It won't seem out of place on the yachts parked in the Bahamas or in the Mediterranean where the Beautiful People spend much time, not to mention money, impressing others. In this Age of Vulgarity . . . it gets harder every day to scale the heights of true vulgarity. But given some loose millions, it can be done — and worse, be admired.'**

We can only surmise what the paper might have thought of 'Diamond Jim' — James Buchanan Brady. His infatuation with those shimmering stones — which set him back $2 million — resulted in thirty sets of diamonds, one for each day of the month, which he wore ostentatiously. The railroads brought him his wealth, but not acceptance by the late-19th century social cognoscenti of Fifth Avenue.

'Money is sweet balm; it heals all wounds.'

ARAB PROVERB

Lady Mary Wortley Montagu, wife of the Ambassador to the court of Constantinople of Sultan Ahmed III in 1716, described a visit to the Sultana Fatima:

> 'Round her neck she wore three chains which reached to her knees: one of large pearls, at the bottom of which hung a fine coloured emerald, as big as a turkey-egg; another, consisting of two hundred emeralds of the more lively green, perfectly matched, every one as large as a half-crown and as thick as three crown pieces; and another of small emeralds, perfectly rounded. But her earrings eclipsed all the rest. They were two diamonds shaped exactly like pears, as large as a big hazel nut . . . her headdress was covered with bodkins of emeralds and diamonds . . . but the piece of luxury which grieved my eyes was the table cloth and napkins, which were all tiffany embroidered with silk and gold . . . it was with the utmost regret that I made use of these costly napkins . . . which were entirely spoilt before dinner was over.'

Gold and precious stones did not look amiss, either, in the sumptuous palaces that the 13th-century Crusaders from Europe found in Constantinople:

> '. . . the palace of Boukoleon was very rich and was made in such a way as I shall tell you. Within this palace . . . there were fully five hundred halls, all connected with one another and all made of gold mosaic . . . and one chapel . . . which was so rich and noble that there was not a hinge nor band nor any other part such as is usually made of iron that was not made of silver, and there was no column that was not of jasper or porphyry or some other rich precious stone. And the pavement was of white marble so smooth and clear that it seemed to be of crystal . . .'

CONQUEST OF CONSTANTINOPLE, ROBERT DE CLARI, c.1200

DEPARTMENT STORES

The most fashionable resort for shopping in London

As wealth increases, so spending it becomes a serious and full-time occupation. The Edwardian period in England was the golden age of an institution created to supply the every need and whim of those afflicted with this problem: the department store. As one visitor to the more opulent examples in London put it, 'Inside, one is immersed in an atmosphere of luxury and pleasure.'
The *Chelsea Herald* of the period reported that in Harrods one found:

> **'. . . everything for a well-ordered household: . . . pyramids of tea and sugar, mountains of coffee . . . mixed with tins of biscuits, breeches' paste, blancmange, glycerine, lobsters, plate powder, sugar candy, boot top powder, wax vestas, salt, prawns, phosphor paste, oysters, milk, knife polish, house flannel, dog biscuits, mustard and a thousand and one other articles . . .'**

Moreover, the store provided clubs for ladies and gentlemen to meet and dine. The decor of the former was in Adams' style, with green silk chairs decorated with appliqué embroidery.

Selfridges provided its clientele with a library and 'silence' room, a bureau de change, post office, savings bank, booking office for railways, steamships and theatres, and a tea garden.

The name most associated with conspicuous consumption, however, has always been New York's Fifth Avenue 'school for taste', Tiffany's. The implicit question asked by its clientele was always: 'What do you have that's new and beautiful today?'

In return — in its heyday — Charles Tiffany sought out art, ornaments and jewellery created by historical as well as modern master craftsmen. The outstanding collection, elegantly displayed, attracted a roll-call of European royalty to his treasure trove, and this seal of approval by Europe's rulers confirmed Tiffany's as the source of the most costly and desirable extravaganzas for generations of Americans.

What could beat a solid silver bicycle, or a solid silver candelabra holding fifty-eight candles; a black pearl necklace; the smouldering 90-facet Kimberley diamond (not for sale); or the ruby that belonged to Catherine the Great; a gold dinner service (bought by J. P. Morgan); or the jewel-like stained glass lamps created by Louis Comfort Tiffany.

For those who 'have everything' but whose desires are still not assuaged, and whose purses remain too full for their comfort, one mail order firm has found the answer. The Neimann Marcus' Catalogue offers a selection of enticing ideas, from a $25 silver-plate baby's bottle and a life-size wooden 'grazing' horse — a snip at $3,000 — to a $21,500 bejewelled chickadee (the state bird of Massachusetts) or a customized 'Cloudhopper' hot air balloon for a mere $18,000.

'All that glitters is sold as gold.'

OGDEN NASH, 20th CENTURY

THE ACQUISITIVE INSTINCT

The acquisitive instinct in man distinguishes us from most other living things . . . except pack-rats and jackdaws. The latter collects bright shining objects; the former lines its nest with an amazing but aimless assortment of things.

Private collections abound; any article is worthy of collection:

Edwardian tin boxes — fishing flies — corkscrews — vintage cars — netsuke — medals — pop memorabilia — porcelain — rare books — autographs — oriental carpets — dolls houses — teddy bears — thimbles — beer mats — cigarette cards — clocks and watches — old wine — writers' scribblings . . .

The idea of the Imperial Easter Egg collection was Peter Carl Fabergé's, a Huguenot expatriate living in St Petersburg. The first was to be a present in 1885 from Tsar Alexander III to his wife. The gold enamelled and bejewelled egg when opened revealed a 'yolk' of pure gold, inside which was a minute golden chick, and, in turn, a tiny ruby egg — the first of a collection of over fifty.

Mrs Hearst once remarked that she regarded the collecting 'mania' of her husband and his friends (who included Mellon and Rockefeller) as a harmless if expensive exercise of vanity which relieved the tension in their crowded working lives.

'What a wretched luxury porcelains are,' complained the diarist Sébastian Mercier in 1771. 'A cat, with one tap of its paw, can do more damage than the devastation of twenty arpents of land.'

Gold enamelled and jewelled table clock in the shape of an Easter egg, created by Michael Perchin in St Petersburg for Tsar Nicholas II.

Two outstanding eclectic collectors had their whims and foibles, as well as their eye for distinguished items, displayed to the world in recent auctions.

The artist Andy Warhol, with his 'mania for collecting', filled his house in New York with the more conventional collector items such as Victorian furniture, works by contemporary artists, jewellery, and Americana, but was unable to resist circus figures and carousels, weather vanes and stuffed animals.

The rock star Elton John, a patron of British football and an enthusiastic collector for 20 years, decided to sell his 'Aladdin's cave' — the contents of his home near Windsor — because it could no longer absorb any more additions.

In addition to valuable paintings, furniture, Art Nouveau and Art Deco items, his collection included an endless array of his own flamboyant costumes worn on tours — including his famous banana collar and outrageous platform shoes — an assortment of eccentric spectacles (which won him the Glass Man of the Year award), and rock and roll records.

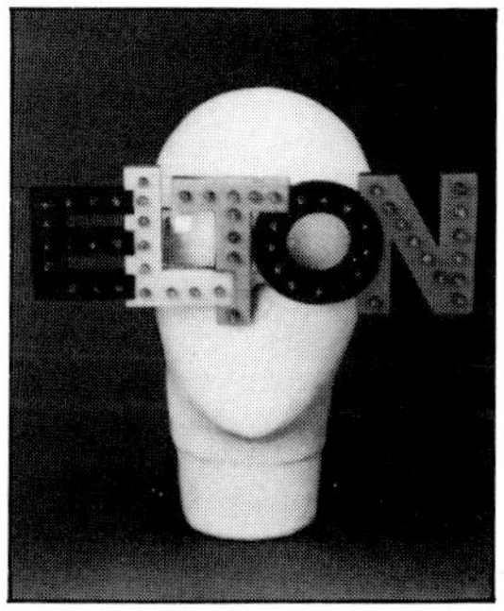

And the hitherto unknown (to the masses) Count Antonio Coluzzi betrayed a weakness known to most men when his collection of 3,000 model trains — and accompanying stations — appeared in its glory at yet another auction room.

For the present-day collector of more prosaic means — the Yuppie, or just the moderately wealthy with an eye for beautiful things — museums are plugging the 'desire gap'.

The British Museum's replica of an Egyptian votive figurine of a cat sells at the rate of at least two a week, at £250 apiece. From the Burrell collection in Glasgow, one can acquire a silver-gilt candlestick for £500, and a ceramic replica collection from the Victoria & Albert Museum can be started with as little as £18.

The desirable replicas of the Metropolitan Museum in New York which make a $3 million profit for the museum include three Dégas dancers, a 4th-century BC 'Mexican' dish, and a model of a Renaissance Florentine horse.

WHIMS AND FANTASIES

'To be truly rich is to possess the means of realising in big ways one's little whims and fantasies and sicknesses . . .

The rich, like other men, are perhaps more simply human than otherwise. But their toys are bigger; they have more of them; they have more of them all at once.'

C. WRIGHT MILLS, 1956

At the turn of the century, Messrs Rolls and Royce found a ready clientele for what was to become the synonym for all that was excellent and beyond the means of the unwealthy man.

Alan Lerner, the American lyricist, who had always wanted to own a Rolls Royce, took Fritz Loewe, his associate composer, down Bond Street in London, with the intention of buying one. Once in the showroom, Fritz became interested: 'You may as well buy one, too,' urged Alan. Fritz succumbed. 'Now, how shall we pay,' Alan asked. 'Don't worry about this one,' Fritz replied, pulling out his cheque book. 'I'll get it. You bought lunch.'

The car continues to be a status symbol. Frank Sinatra's wedding present to his fourth wife Barbara was a peacock blue $100,000 Rolls Royce. Her present to him, for the same price, was a grey Jaguar.

And the 'children' of the 1980s' financial boom in London found their status symbols in Porsches and BMWs.

The yacht was — and remains — a powerful symbol of wealth, providing a languid playground for the rich.

ALIE

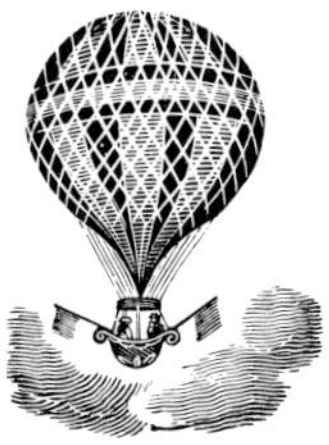

GETTING AWAY FROM IT ALL

SENECA 1st CENTURY AD

'Men travel widely to different sorts of places seeking different distractions . . . always seeking after something which eludes them.'

Wealthy Romans had the entire Mediterranean world to choose from when deciding where to spend their holidays. Good roads, carriages and inns abounded.

A popular destination was the Bay of Naples, and in particular Baiae, where the rich and the dissolute repaired for days of idleness and sybaritic existence. The wealthier had villas scattered along the hillside overlooking the bay, with their swimming pools, fountains, and cool marble courtyards.

Seneca, however, was scornful:

> **'I made the best of Baiae . . . but left the day after I arrived. Can you imagine . . . living in a bijou villa and keeping tally of the unfaithful wives sailing by, of the gaily painted craft . . . of the roses bobbing on every lagoon . . . and listening to the nocturnal caterwauling of those who felt moved to song?'**

The travelling wealthy English Milords of the 18th century had no less exuberant tastes when in Paris, to the distaste of Lord Chesterfield, that great connoisseur of the grand tour. Travelling with a tutor or guide, and possibly valet, lackey, coachman and footman, the ostensible reason for the tour was to gain social graces, learn the languages and become educated in the mores, manners and arts of the Continent. However, reality was often more down to earth.

> **'As soon as they rise, which is very late, they breakfast together, to the utter loss of two good morning hours. Then they go by coachfuls to the Palais, the Invalides and Notre Dame; from thence to the English coffee house, where they make up their tavern party for dinner. From dinner, where they drink quick, they adjourn in clusters to the play, where they crowd up the stage, drest [sic] up in very fine clothes, very ill made by a Scotch or Irish tailor. From the play to the tavern again where they get very drunk and where they either quarrel among themselves or sally forth, commit some riot in the**

A tour to foreign parts, 1778.

streets and are taken up by the watch . . . their tender vows are addressed to their Irish laundress, unless by chance some itinerant English-woman, eloped from her husband or her creditors, defrauds her of them.'

LORD CHESTERFIELD, LETTERS TO HIS SON

In the latter part of the 20th century, it is hard to escape from the enticing invitations to escape the social, work and time pressures we have willed upon ourselves, and dream of far-flung shores.

For those with enough money, a miniscule island dropped into the expanse of the Indian Ocean or Caribbean provides a paradise on earth.

George Cruikshank

HELP IS AT HAND

One of the great joys of possessing wealth has always been to employ others to look after one's every need and whim.

In 1825, the husband and wife team of Samuel and Sarah Adams produced a 'Practical Guide to the Peculiar Duties and Business of all descriptions of Servants' for those new to the business.

Quoting Francis Bacon: 'that he who would live even with the world should calculate his Expenses at half his Income, and he who would grow Rich, at one-third', they proceed to offer a Rule for a Gentleman on how to appropriate a large income:

'Viz . . . 33 per cent or one-third for household Expenses, including provisions and all other articles of household consumption;
. . . 25 per cent or one-fourth for servants and equipage including horses, carriages and liveries;
. . . 25 per cent or one-fourth for clothes, education of children, medical assistance, pocket, private and extra expenses; including entertainment;
. . . 12½ per cent or one-eighth for rent, taxes and repairs of house and furniture;
. . . 4½ per cent as a reserve for contingencies.

They then offer their readers advice on the number and type of servants needed by various households. For example:

Income per annum
£100 or guineas A widow or other unmarried lady may keep a young maid servant at a low salary, say from 5-10 guineas.
About £200 A gentleman and lady without children. A professed servant maid of all work, from 12-14 guineas.
£500-£600 A gentleman and lady with children. Three females and one man; viz. a cook, house maid and a nursery maid, or other female servant; with a livery servant, as groom and footman. A gardner occasionally.
£1,500-£2,000 Ditto. Six female and five men servants, viz. a cook, housekeeper, two house maids, kitchen maid, and nursery maid, or other female servant; with a coachman, groom, footman, gardner, and an assistant in the garden and stable.
£4,000-£5,000 Ditto. Eleven female and thirteen male servants, viz. a housekeeper, cook, Lady's maid, nurse, two house maids, laundry maid, still-room maid, nursery maid, kitchen maid, and scullion, with butler, valet, house steward, coachman, two grooms, one assistant, two footmen, three gardners and a labourer.

A HANDFUL OF PHILANTHROPISTS

Several generations of wealthy American families have been seriously involved in endowing research and educational institutions and foundations, museums and art galleries, libraries and universities, housing for the poor, welfare for children, urban redevelopment, medical programmes, travel opportunities. They have become household names: Ford . . . Mellon . . . Rockefeller . . . Carnegie . . . Guggenheim . . . du Pont . . . Getty . . . Kellogg.

Andrew Carnegie had two great passionate causes in his life, after making his millions in steel: he endowed libraries and educational institutions in the UK and the US with tens of millions of dollars. 'A taste for reading', he asserted, 'is one of the most precious possessions of life. I would much rather be instrumental in bringing to the working man or woman this taste than mere dollars.'

THE MACMILLION.

It prompted his compatriot in wealth, Henry Frick — for whom Fragonards were infinitely more precious — to wonder 'why give libraries to all those small towns which only end up going bust trying to keep them running?'

The trustees of the many institutions founded and endowed by him with a vision to achieve his objectives thus found in their terms of endowment his oft-repeated words: 'I have therefore transferred $10 million 5% first mortgage bonds of the United States Steel Corporation to . . .'

Carnegie also hoped 'to hasten the abolition of international wars, the foulest blot of our civilisation'.

His total gifts and bequests totalled over $330 million.

Carnegie's contemporary, J. D. Rockefeller, was advised in matters of philanthropy by Frederick Gates. 'Your fortune,' he told him, 'is rolling up, rolling up like an avalanche. You must keep up with it . . . you must distribute it faster

than it grows. If you do not, it will crush you and your children and your children's children.'

Three generations of Rockefellers have since given over $1 thousand million to various institutions and foundations, including the Rockefeller Foundation.

The Florentine Medici family were one of the greatest patrons in Renaissance Italy.

The 'founder' of the family, Cosimo de Medici, made his fortune in banking, and spent lavishly on charities, arts and learning. It was his grandson, Lorenzo de Medici, whose name is primarily associated with the arts, and whose patronage gave us the masterpieces of Sandro Botticelli, Ghirlandaio, Filippino Lippi, Andrea Verrocchio and Michelangelo.

In the UK, Quaker businessmen have been notable in their donations to 'charities': The Cadburys and the Rowntrees — two Quaker families whose fortunes grew as incomes and a growing taste for chocolate coincided in late 19th-century England — found themselves in a dilemma. The pursuit of wealth was encouraged by Victorian Quakers, but personal accumulation was a contradiction to the 'simple life' which is an intrinsic part of the Quaker ethos.

Distribution was the solution. The legacy of these two families are the many grant-making trusts in their names, established to further a variety of social, religious and educational causes including housing, alcoholism, health and handicap, penal affairs and peace and race relations.

THREE WOMEN PATRONS

In Mantua, in the late 15th century, Isabella d'Este was supporting and encouraging writers and artists whose works she avidly collected, and who included Titian, Andrea Mantegna and Carravagio.

Her 'namesake' of 400 years later, Isabella Gardner, established and endowed one of the great North American galleries of Renaissance art — Fenway Court in Boston — with the money of her financier husband, Jack.

A third woman patron — Peggy Guggenheim — created a lively abstract expressionist art gallery in her home on Venice's Grand Canal, while her uncle Solomon Guggenheim's foundation created the spectacular modern art gallery on New York's Fifth Avenue, designed by Frank Lloyd Wright.

THE SEARCH FOR IMMORTALITY

Of the American art-collecting fraternity at the turn of the century, many endowed museums with their private collections. Their motives may not always have been pure, but there is no doubt who has gained by their wealth and generosity.

One man was the mastermind behind this move — Joseph Duveen, the spectacular art dealer who spanned the turn of the 19th and 20th centuries. His secretary, N. S. Berhman, has left his interpretation of Duveen's 'masterpiece':

> 'Duveen's career had a beautiful composition. Early in the century he inherited from his Uncle Henry three gigantic clients: Morgan, Altman and P. A. B. Widener — and thereafter time, and the swelling American prosperity supplied new ones. There were great millionaires who spent little and small millionaires who spent vast sums . . .'

However:

> 'Duveen was keenly sensitive to social change, and he saw before most people did that, between them, income taxes and inheritance taxes were going to make it impossible for men of wealth to buy art for themselves or leave collections to their heirs. The public bequest, impervious to taxation, was the way out. Specifically, the public bequest of 'Duveens' was the way out. By earmarking his purchases for a museum, a collector could afford to buy art: at least, he could let the art pass through his hands on the way to the museums from Duveen. Gifts to museums offered his clients not merely economy but immortality. Using Duveen's method, an aged American millionaire could, in good conscience, circumvent oblivion and the collector of Internal Revenue at a single stroke. Under Duveen's spell, one after another of his clients — H. E. Huntington, Frick, Mellon, Bache, Kress — took up this form of philanthropy.'

N. S. BEHRMAN, DUVEEN (1953)

IDIOSYNCHRATIC TALES

FRANCIS BACON, 16th/17th CENTURY

'Money is like muck; not good unless it be spread.'

. . . Divorce Bel-Air style: an $11 million account plus a monthly allowance of $5,000 for groceries, $3,300 for dinners, $1,200 for lunches, $10,000 for dinner parties and $25,000 for clothing and other accessories. The family name: Keck, oil-rich and heirs to one of California's largest grant-making foundations.

. . . The most expensive ever first-night coiffure: an Elizabeth Taylor extravaganza topped with diamonds and a nine-carat gold rose, for the first night of *Taming of the Shrew* in Paris, 1967. Cost: $428,000.

. . . a Duke of Sutherland who used to pin £1,000 banknotes on his wife's pillow.

. . . a Daily Telegraph advertisement in 1901, to solicitors: 'If among your clients you have . . . a lady who is willing to purchase the rank of peeress for £25,000, paid in cash to her future husband, I shall be pleased if you will communicate with . . .'

. . . the miserly millionaire Commodore Vanderbilt, who refused a bottle of champagne when mortally ill, asking 'won't sody water do instead?'

. . . Prince de Conti who, when his gift of a diamond worth 5,000 lire was spurned by his lady love, had it pulverised and the dust sprinkled over her written rejection.

. . . the dinner in Delmonico's in New York where cigarettes rolled in hundred-dollar bills were passed round after coffee.

. . . an Austro-Hungarian count who would scatter gold sovereigns at racecourses — after happily losing £5,000 — saying to those trying to retrieve them: 'keep them, I've finished with them — I'll get some more tomorrow.'

. . . Marechal Richelieu who, when his grandson refused a gift of a purse filled with gold, flung it out of the window saying: 'Let the street cleaner have it, then.'

. . . Mrs Eva Stotesbury, defending the gold-plated taps in her home in Florida, claimed simply that 'it saves so much polishing'.

. . . a rich American for whom Asprey's made a gold toothbrush, with a nine carat telescopic handle and pure bristle head, all reducing to the size of a pillbox — to clean his teeth after business lunches. It became a best seller.

A MORAL TALE

FRANCIS BACON, APOPHTHEGMUS (1625)

'There was one that found a great mass of money digging under the ground in his grandfather's house: and being somewhat doubtful of the use, signified it to the emperor that he had found such treasure. The emperor made a rescript thus: 'use it'. He writ back again that the sum was greater than his estate or condition could use. The emperor writ a new rescript thus: 'abuse it'.'

CHAPTER 8

BETTING AND GAMBLING

'Gaming is an enchanting witchery, gotten between idleness and vice . . .'

CHARLES COTTON, THE COMPLEAT GAMESTER, 1674

The attraction of gambling – the quest for the hazardous, the unknown and the daring, the desire for victory, the love of gain, and the fascination of acquiring wealth instantaneously – has accompanied man for countless centuries. Modern theories as to why it is such a strong instinct mention chance and probability as being endemic in our lives anyway; or stress our frustration at our individual choices being increasingly curtailed in the societies we live in.

Games of chance, lotteries, horse-racing, dice or roulette – each in their own way offer an unpredictability against which, accompanied by that elusive deity called luck, individuals can test themselves . . . and gain or lose that magical substance called money in the process.

> **'Gambling . . . is taken up as a quicker road to wealth than by pursuing honest industry, and everyone engaged in it, be it dabbling on the stock exchange, betting on horse racing or otherwise, hopes to win . . . it is a disease that is most contagious . . .'**
>
> *J. ASHTON, HISTORY OF GAMBLING IN ENGLAND*

A ROCKY OUTCROP IN MONACO

'Everybody had money then, and knew how to lose it.'

PAUL DE KETCHIVA, CROUPIER AT THE CASINO IN MONTE CARLO, REMINISCING IN 1910 ON HOW THINGS HAD BEEN

The brothers Blanc ran a highly successful casino in Hesse-Homburg before being invited by the destitute Prince Charles III to take over his local failing establishment in Monaco in 1862.

THE GAMBLING ROOMS AT MONTE CARLO "RIEN NE VA PLUS"

The Casino had its code of honour for those whose luck ran out: the viatique (the fare home), somewhat flamboyantly applied.

> 'If you apply to the Administration you have got to swear that you have lost over £300 [calculated at over £10,000 at 1980s prices]; they will then take you round the rooms like a criminal in order that the croupiers at the tables where you have played may identify you and confirm your statement . . . After this you are photographed and once more taken round to be shown to all the doorkeepers, who are then given orders not to admit you any more. Next, you have to sign a promissory note for the amount of your travelling expenses, and instead of giving you money you are told that an employee of the establishment will meet you at the station at such and such an hour and hand you a second-class ticket to your destination.'
>
> *TEN DAYS AT MONTE CARLO, 1898*

Gambling systems became the rage by the end of the 19th century. A Parisian reader of the *New York Herald* even invited 'any of your readers to go into partnership with me for a month at the Monte Carlo tables. I have discovered a system . . .'

In Edwardian times, some gamblers at the casino employed 'cruder' — if more pleasurable — means of acquiring luck . . . and money. They adopted 'mascots' — pretty girls — who charged gamblers 25 per cent of their winnings for bringing luck. One girl was reputed to have earned £3,000 in one week alone.

At about the same time other gamblers adopted several winning strategies. One used a pet spider: placed in a matchbox painted half red and half black, if the spider emerged from the red end, the gambler backed the red, and if from the black, he backed the black.

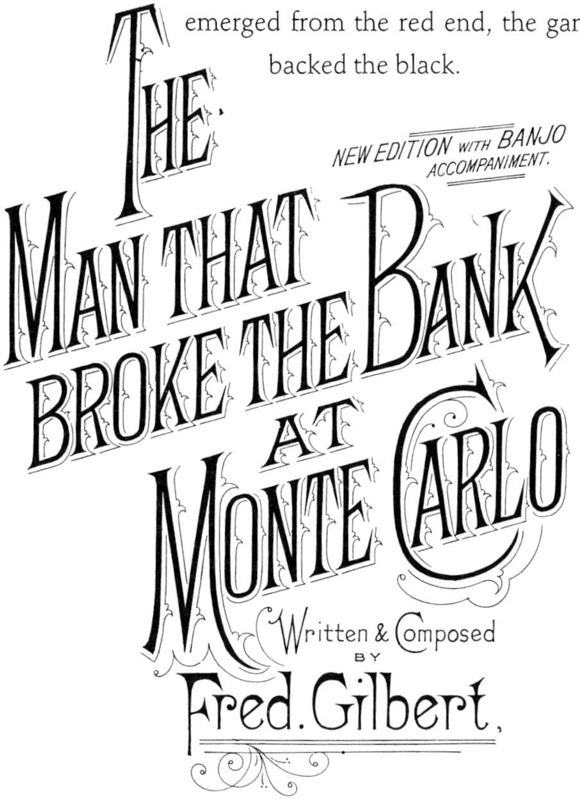

Charles Deville Wells was a British engineer, 'a common little man', who claimed an infallible system. In 1892, he broke the bank several times in three days. Boxes of gold coins had to be brought in to resuscitate the empty bank, and in the meantime the roulette table was covered with black crêpe — a publicity stunt which more than paid off!

Stunts at the gambling tables was a method also used by André Citroen, the French car manufacturer. One of his better-known efforts was by playing baccarat one night in 1926 for the sole purpose of losing — and making it one of the biggest losing sessions at 13 million francs. Banks were called in to save Citroen as his personal wealth disappeared, and he was heard to say:

> **'I am not the least interested in the game, nor in whether I win or lose. I am only interested in whether or not the amount is large enough to be noticed.'**

GAMBLING LADIES

'Faro: gambling played with a pack of fifty-two cards. First played in France and England, Faro was especially popular in US gaming houses in the 19th century. Players indicate on the table — which is marked with representations of the thirteen cards of the spade suit — the card they believe will win or lose. The dealer then takes one card, called the soda, from the dealing box. This card is not used. The second card drawn loses, and third card wins.'

In 18th-century England, ladies of 'position' enjoyed a certain notoriety by opening their own homes to gambling — in particular for Faro. Lady Buckingham, the most notorious of these ladies, slept with a blunderbuss and a pair of pistols by her bedside, to protect her Faro bank. One night, however, the cash box was mysteriously spirited away and rumours abounded of other items which had disappeared from her home during Faro sessions. The *Times* of the day gave daily accounts of these social occasions in the houses of Her Ladyship and her two 'faro sisters', Lady Luttrell and Mrs Sturt.

10 February 1793
'The profits of Faro are become so considerably reduced that most of the banks now lose almost every evening, after defraying the expenses of the house . . . those public spirited ladies who give such frequent routs, do so at a certain gain . . . the punters at Mrs Hobart's and Mrs Sturt's Faro banks have dropped off considerably'

2 May 1793
'A Banking Lady, in St James Square, is about to commence a prosecution, because it is said that there was much filching at her Faro table. The house was quite in uproar on Tuesday night'

4 April 1794
'It is impossible to conceive a more complete system of fraud and dishonour than is practised every night at the Faro banks. Though every table has four croupiers . . . double that number are necessary to watch all the little tricks and artifices of some of the fashionable punters'

The gambling instinct will not be crushed. George Cruikshank packs his 1853 satirical print with the follies of attempting to do so.

s want to spoil our Sport; Shut up our "Betting-Shops" & destroy our Counters! (cries of
th our own Spades! but we'll see if Diamond carn't Cut Diamond? (Hear! hear
But there is one Card, (a Picture Card) who has been writing what he calls a
Cuts, in which he tries to persuade people to leave off Betting altogether (Oh! oh!
!) Yes this Card, not only wants Betting & Gambling to be done away with but
s to be Honest! (oh! oh! with much laughter & cries of Humbug!) Yes! not only that,
er as well as Honest!!! (Oh! oh! oh! with shouts of laughter – Stuff & nonsense &
is name is George Cruikshank! (great disapprobation!) Yes Gents, this is going a great
Now the Point is, how are we to "Play our Cards"? Why we must go to Parliament"! there are
"Lords & Commons" who "Play" & "Bet" & Keep the Horses that we carry on our trade
Lords & Gentlemen, the Nobs of the Aristocracy to countenance the Betting system, why
at we may turn-up our noses at honest "Pumps" & go on with our
Game of "Beggar my Neighbour"! (Hear! hear! & loud Cheering

vide report of ye Packed meeting

ls" of the Betting-Shop interest to consider & adopt the best

a humble attempt in the "Pre Raphael" Style by George Cruikshank

THE TURF

In 16th-century England, 'prizes' for winning horse-races were silver bells. Later, guineas were attached to them. By the end of the 17th century, gold cups were offered as prizes, each worth 100 guineas or more.

The racetrack has always been seen as a stage for those hoping to turn the art of horse-riding into a scientific horse-racing formula.

In the early 1900s, the gentlemen of the track received the following circular from a woman bookmaker:

> **'Gentlemen in quest of reliable racing intelligence are invited to communicate with Miss . . . . . Only those who are prepared to pay well need apply, as Miss . . . . . is not one of those who gives away tips.**
>
> **During the latter part of the 1903 flat racing season Miss . . . . . decided to commence business as a racing adviser and she at once met with conspicuous success, and invites all sportsmen in quest of genuine racing intelligence to join her list of regular wire subscribers. Satisfaction guaranteed to all regular subscribers.'**

The anti-lobby saw gambling as

> **'. . . a social cancer, eating into the vitals of the nation'**

and lamented the fact that

> **'. . . so noble an animal as the horse should be made the unconscious medium of such a degrading passion as gambling.'**

Regardless of punters' delusions, the bookmakers were simply in the business of making money. One of them penned his thoughts:

> 'Now listen. I have attended every race meeting held in the land over and over again. I am as well known in sporting circles as any man could possibly be . . . my betting transactions amount to thousands and thousands . . .
>
> Let me candidly and tactfully tell you that I have never known a backer of horses to succeed permanently. The backer is successful so long as his money, pluck and luck last, or until ruin overtakes him . . .
>
> He diligently studies all kinds of plans and systems; he also fools his money away with 'tipsters' — a set of race-course harpies . . . He tries first and second favourites, newspaper naps, jockey mounts . . . some of his own particular fancy, and some of other people's. He gluts over sporting news, and talks of owners, trainers and jockeys in a most familiar style as though they were his own personal friends! He becomes acquainted with horses' names and pedigrees, and eventually his mind is so full of Turf matter that business, his occupation and employment become of second importance; he sacrifices house, comfort, occupation and money — what for? In the hope of making easy money, but in the end for the benefit of the bookmakers.'

THE DELUDED SPORTSMAN, BY A BOOKMAKER (1890)

THE CURRENCY QUESTION; OR, THE STOCK EXCHANGE OUT FOR THE DAY.

Jones. "I SAY, BROWN, THINGS ARE DEUCED BAD IN THE CITY."
Brown. "THEN I'M DEUCED GLAD I'M AT EPSOM!"

LOTTERIES

The first known lottery in England was held in the reign of Elizabeth I. The prizes offered were of such value that participating in lotteries became a means for a citizen to become truly wealthy – while avoiding the disapproval normally shown to those who hankered after yet more gold and silver. The draws could last for weeks, and prizes might include 'a silver table service . . . tapestries finely worked with gold . . . bedsteads with velvet draperies . . . rare bureaux and cabinets . . . fine clothing . . .' enough to furnish a home handsomely.

Everyone participated, regardless of means and social class. What each participant planned to do with his winnings is not known; but one footman (footmen, it seems, were more prone than others to succumb to this 'vice') who disposed of his entire savings of the previous twenty years on two lottery tickets – and which failed to be drawn – was driven to suicide. On his death, a note was found in his box on how he planned to spend his newly acquired wealth:

> 'As soon as I have received the money, I will marry Grace Towers; but as she has been cross and coy, I will keep her as a servant. Every morning she shall get me a mug of strong beer, with toast, nutmeg and sugar in it; then I will sleep till ten, after which I will have a large sack posset. My dinner shall be on table by one, and never without a good pudding. I will have a stock of wine and brandy laid in. About five in the afternoon I

will have tarts and jellies, and a gallon bowl of punch; at ten, a hot supper of two dishes. If I am in a good humour, and Grace behaves herself, she shall sit down with me. To bed about twelve.'

The first 'state' lottery in England to be authorised by Parliament was held in 1694, to raise a loan of £1 million. The shares were of £10 each, and contributors were entitled to annuities for sixteen years, appropriated from certain salt and beer duties named in the Act.

A second lottery was authorised three years later; but within two years, virtue got the better of the authorities, because

'. . . several evil-disposed persons have set up many mischievous and unlawful games, called lotteries . . . and have thereby got to themselves great sums of money from children and servants of several gentlemen, traders and merchants and from other unwary persons, to the utter ruin and impoverishment of many families and to the reproach of the English laws and government . . .'

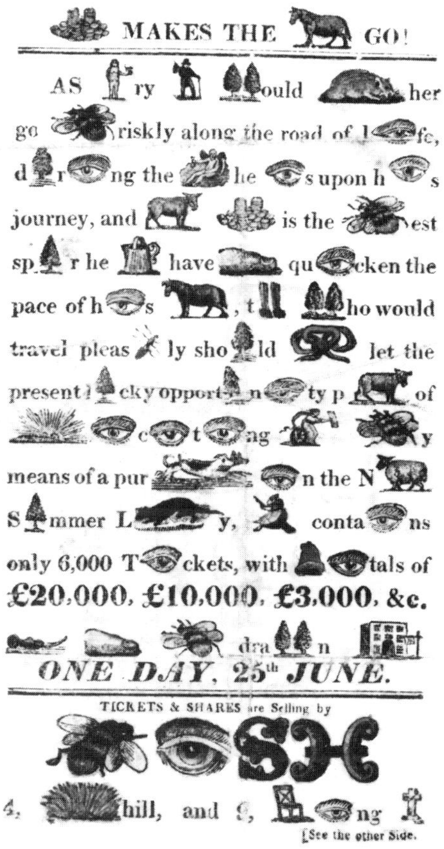

Virtue was short-lived, however, and the art of lotteries reached its peak in England in the 18th century, becoming a regular expedient for raising money to meet state expenditure.

The art of advertising lotteries was perfected by a Mr. T. Bish. With his partner, a respectable stockbroker, he opened offices in Cornhill – not far from the other famous lottery house of Richardson, uniquely placed opposite the Bank of England.

SOME UNUSUAL WAGERS

The famous White's betting book, kept at the London club between 1743 and 1877, contains a selection of bets that its members indulged in: the first in the book, for 100 guineas, was that 'the Dowager Duchess of Marlborough outlives the Dowager Duchess of Cleveland'.

The slightest difference of opinion was sufficient for odds to be laid. The last bet noted in the book, for a mere £25, was 'that this country is at war with some European power on or before this day six months'.

In the intervening years, wagers covered births, deaths and marriages, as well as the outcome of lotteries, and future political events.

Richard Steele, the editor of *The Spectator* and a member of Whites, said in 1801:

> 'There is nothing, however trivial or ridiculous, which is not capable of producing a bet.
>
> Many pounds have been lost upon the colour of a coach horse, an article in the news or a change in the weather . . .'

Another writer lamented the constant recourse to wagers:

> 'The management of a dispute was formerly attempted by reason and argument, but the new way of adjusting all difference in opinion is by the sword or the wager, so that the only method of decision is to risk a thousand pounds, or to take the chance of being run through the body . . .'

> 'I have frequently observed, in the course of my researches, the strange methods and customs peculiar to gaming, horse racing, dice and wagers; the latter are governed by whim and extreme folly . . . In 1729 a Poulterer of Leadenhall Market betted £50 he would walk 202 times round the area of Upper Moorfields in 27 hours, and accordingly proceeded at the rate of five miles

an hour on the amusing pursuit, to the infinite improvement of his business, and great edification of hundreds of spectators. Wagers are now a favourite custom with too many of the Londoners; they very frequently, however, originate over the bottle or the porter pot.'

MALCOLM'S ANECDOTES OF THE MANNERS AND CUSTOMS OF LONDON DURING THE EIGHTEENTH CENTURY

. . . Sir John Packington (in the reign of Queen Elizabeth I), £3,000 for a race against three other noblemen, swimming from Westminster Bridge to Greenwich. The Queen intervened and the race was abandoned.

. . . Casanova recalled in his memoires: 20,000 guineas that the Chevalier d'Eon (formerly the French ambassador in London) was in fact a woman. Since it could only be decided if d'Eon himself agreed to be examined in the presence of witnesses — on the offer of half the stakes — and he refused, the bet was withdrawn.

. . . the writer Horace Walpole in a letter (1750): 'They have put in the papers a good story made on White's; a man dropped down dead at the door, was carried in; the club immediately made bets whether he was dead or not, and when they were going to bleed him, the wagerers for his death interposed, and said it would affect the fairness of the bet.'

. . . Charles James Fox in 1755 with Lord Bolingbroke, one guinea on condition of paying £1,000 when the debts of the country amounted to £171 million . . . which occurred some years later.

. . . on the last illness of Louis XIV of France in August 1715, Lord Stair, English ambassador in France, 'with the flair and genius of that nation' (Voltaire) wagered the king would not live beyond September. The bet was won. The king died on 1 September.

. . . £1,500 that a man could live twelve hours under water. A 'desperate fellow' was hired and sunk in a ship . . . neither of which subsequently resurfaced.

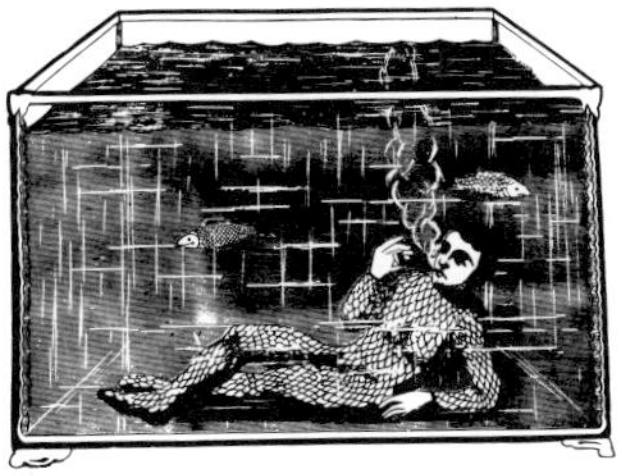

Spending and gambling can result in financial disaster all too often, as described by William Hazlitt in the 19th century:

> 'It is hard to be without money. To get on without it is like travelling in a foreign country without a passport – you are stopped, suspected and much ridiculed at every turn, besides being subjected to the most serious inconveniences. The want of money that I here allude to is not altogether that which arises from absolute poverty... but the uncertain, casual, precarious mode of existence in which the temptation to spend remains after the means are exhausted, the want of money joined with the hope and possibility of getting it, the intermediate state of difficulty and suspense between the last guinea or shilling and the next that we have the good luck to encounter... What luxury, what a God's-send in such a dilemma, to find a half-crown which has slipped through a hole in the lining of your waistcoat, a crumpled banknote in your breeches pocket, or a guinea clinking in the bottom of your trunk, which has been thoughtlessly left there out of a former heap! Vain hope! Unfounded illusion!...'

WILLIAM HAZLITT, ON THE WANT OF MONEY (1827)